Sew Baby

First published in 2018

Search Press Limited
Wellwood, North Farm Road,
Tunbridge Wells, Kent TN2 3DR

Photographs by Garie Hind

ISBN: 978-1-78221-459-5

Suppliers
For details of suppliers, please visit
the Search Press website:
www.searchpress.com

For further inspiration, visit Debbie's
website: www.debbieshore.co.uk

Printed in China by 1010 Printing
International Ltd

Safety advice

The projects in this book have been
photographed to show them to their
best advantage – always refer to current
government guidelines for baby health, safety
and sleeping advice.

Never leave baby unattended: all babies were
constantly supervised during photography.

Please take extra care when sewing seams
or sewing on items such as beads or buttons.
If you are in any doubt about the strength of
your stitching, remove any swallowable parts.

Sew Baby

20 cute and colourful projects for the home, the nursery and on the go

Debbie Shore

SEARCH PRESS

Contents

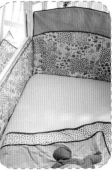

Contents

Cot Pocket,
page 50

Insulated Bottle Bag,
page 54

Patchwork Pillow,
page 56

Quiet Cube,
page 86

Cot Quilt,
page 88

Burp Cloths,
page 92

Introduction

I used to love decorating the nursery when my children were babies. I made colourful furnishings and tactile play areas, quilts and blankets to snuggle up with, and calm and comfortable areas for baby (and me!) at sleep time. Now that I'm a grandma, I'm enjoying making these things all over again! I've filled this book with ideas for the nursery, practical storage solutions and bags of ideas for baby-on-the-go. From simple, useful items such as the Bandana Bib (see page 40) and Travel Changing Mat (see page 82), to projects that can really save you money, like the Baby Nest (see page 42) and Stroller Sleeping Bag (see page 78).

Making beautiful, affordable things for baby is both enjoyable and satisfying, but the most rewarding feeling is giving a unique gift for new parents to treasure, which in time they can then pass on to the next new member of the family!

I've added QR-coded videos to this book to help you with some of the techniques. To view the videos, you'll need a smartphone and a QR code reader application (the majority of these are free). Once you've installed it, use the phone's camera to scan the code, which will automatically load the video...

Debbie x

10 tips for the complete beginner

1 Start with a simple project such as the Cot Pocket (page 50) or Knotted Headband (page 14). As your skills grow you'll feel confident to tackle more advanced projects like the Baby Nest (page 42) or Stroller Bag (page 68).

2 Make up your project in inexpensive fabric first. That way, if things go wrong you're not wasting anything but time!

3 As the saying goes, measure twice cut once! Stitches can be unpicked but if you don't cut the right size there's little you can do.

4 Reverse a couple of stitches at the start and end of your sewing line. Some machines have a 'fix' stitch that puts three or four tiny stitches close together. This will stop the stitches coming undone.

5 Cut your fabric pieces on the grain – this means that the weave of the fabric sits vertically and horizontally; if you cut at an angle your fabric could twist.

6 To help you sew in a straight line and create even seam allowances, place a strip of masking tape over the bed of your sewing machine as a guide for your fabric (an elastic band around the free arm works well too). Measure from the needle 5mm (¼in) to the right and place your tape at this point. Seam allowances are 5mm (¼in) unless otherwise stated.

7 Topstitching can be a bit daunting, so sew slowly. If you're not very confident, use a thread that matches your fabric so that it doesn't stand out too much.

8 Pin at right angles to the edge of your fabric. You'll find the layers don't slip and, although you should be taking out your pins as you sew, if the needle accidentally hits a pin there is less chance of either breaking.

9 Change your sewing-machine needle regularly. It is recommended you put a new needle in after every eight hours of sewing – you'll notice a difference to the stitches and even the sound of your machine! It's always good form when you change the needle to take off the needle plate and clean out any lint. (Take a look at your manufacturer's instructions.)

10 Relax! Sewing is fun! Don't worry if things go a bit wrong – put your work down and come back to it the next day. It won't seem half as bad as you first thought!

Materials & tools

Fabrics

Choosing fabrics for the nursery is so enjoyable and, of course, it's entirely down to your personal taste! From soft muted pastels to bold prints, choose fabrics themed with anything from animals to cartoon characters. Bear in mind how long you want your projects to last though: those cute baby curtains may not be appreciated by a five-year-old!

I prefer cotton fabric as it's breathable, soft, has a good drape and washes well; pre-wash fabric that will need to be laundered to avoid shrinkage.

Fleece is a lovely fabric for sleeping bags and snuggly blankets – it doesn't fray, making it easy to work with, and it's available in many colours and prints.

Threads

Try to use the same composition as your fabric: cotton for cotton, polyester for man-made, silk for silk. It's worth investing in the best-quality thread you can afford, as you'll find your seams are stronger and you end up with less lint in your machine.

Wadding/batting

This is the layer of padding put in between two pieces of fabric to give structure, warmth and a luxurious feel to a project. It can be made from many different fibres: cotton, polyester, silk and wool bamboo, to name a few, and sometimes several fibres are mixed together. The big decision is choosing a type. A lot depends on what you're using it for, and whether the item will be washed. As we're talking babies in this book, the probability is that whatever you're making will at some point need to be laundered, so choose a wadding/batting that won't shrink. I like natural, organic, untreated fibres for breathability and softness, and prefer types that are fire-retardant. The 'loft' refers to the thickness of the wadding/batting: the higher the loft the thicker the wadding/batting. Low loft is preferred for quilting, while high loft would make a very cosy sleeping bag!

Fusible fleece gives structure to bags and is simply ironed onto the wrong side of your fabric – some types contain thermal threads, making them perfect for insulating bottle bags.

When choosing toy filler, look for high-loft, super-soft toy filler that is washable and flame-retardant.

Sewing machine

For the projects in this book you won't need a top-of-the-range machine, but a range of stitches and feet are always useful. You'll need to be able to drop the feed dogs and use a darning foot for free-motion embroidery, and a walking foot is helpful if you're sewing through several layers of fabric, for instance with the cot quilt.

Rotary cutter, ruler and mat

Well worth the investment, these tools will help you measure and cut accurately and quickly – particularly useful for larger projects like the Baby Nest (page 42), or where accuracy is important, as with the patchwork Cot Quilt and Bumper (pages 88 and 46). The most popular cutter size is 45mm; go for the largest mat and ruler you have space for!

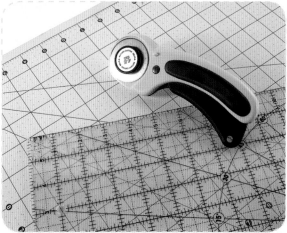

Scissors

Dressmaking shears that are used just for fabrics are a must-have, along with a small pair to snip threads, plus paper scissors. Pinking shears will help to stop your fabric from fraying and create a zigzag effect on felt.

Adhesives

A repositionable fabric spray for appliqué, permanent fabric glue spray that adheres when ironed, and a strong wet glue are my essentials. Spray glues that make wadding/batting fusible are also a great tool.

Marking tools

There are lots of options available to you. Air-erasable pens deliver ink that disappears after a few hours, while water-erasable ink washes away. I tend to use heat-erasable ink pens in the seam allowance – the ink will disappear using either friction or heat from the iron. Fabric pencils are useful and are available in both light and dark colours so they stand out against any fabric. Chalk is an option, but I find it can be difficult to make an accurate mark.

Useful stitches

Machine stitches

STRAIGHT STITCH

This is the most used stitch on any project, taking the top and bottom thread on your machine through two or more layers of fabric to form a straight, single-line seam. Lengthen the thread to create a tacking/basting stitch, and shorten the length of the stitch when making smaller or three-dimensional projects such as the Balloon Mobile (page 32), as the small stitches will be strong when put under the strain of stuffing.

TRIPLE STRAIGHT STITCH

This stitch won't crack when used on stretch fabric, and makes a bold outline when used as a decorative stitch. The needle will jump backwards then forwards to create a backstitch.

ZIGZAG STITCH

A decorative stitch that can be used to join two pieces of fabric together to create a flat seam, this stitch can also be useful to help stop the raw edges of your fabric from fraying. Shorten the length of the stitch to make a satin stitch. Perfect for appliqué, use this for the Laundry Bin (page 58) if you don't want to use free-motion embroidery.

OVEREDGE STITCH

Similar to an overlocking stitch, this is designed to take the thread slightly over the raw edge of your fabric to stop it from fraying. Use this on items that may wear or need to be laundered, and if you sell your items this gives a professional finish.

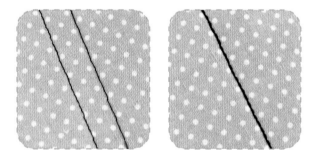 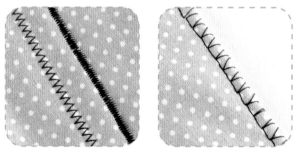

Decorative stitches

The number of decorative stitches varies from machine to machine, depending on manufacturer and price point. These stitches add pretty borders and finishing touches to your projects, or can simply be embroidered onto ribbon or tape to make embellishments such as bows.

Hand stitches

SLIP STITCH

I use this to finish off bias binding. Keep the stitch to a short length and try to catch just a couple of strands of the fold of the bias binding to keep the stitch as invisible as possible. (See bias binding on page 12.)

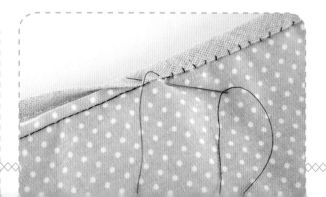

LADDER STITCH

This is the perfect stitch for closing turning gaps or making repairs in seams. Take the needle from one side of the opening to the opposite side, then gently pull to close the gap. Small stitches are the least visible.

RUNNING STITCH

Tiny running stitches can be a strong as a machine straight stitch; use longer stitches for tacking/basting.

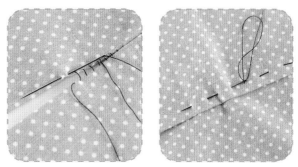

Free-motion embroidery

This type of embroidery is so popular and loads of fun! Think of your needle and thread as a pen and ink, but instead of moving the pen over the paper, you move the fabric under the needle to doodle and create your own unique designs. You'll need a machine with a drop feed dog facility – the feed dogs are the teeth that carry the fabric through the machine, and dropping these out of the way gives you control of moving the fabric in any direction you like. You'll also need a free-motion or darning foot – this foot 'hops' across the fabric and allows you to see where you're stitching. Some sewing machines come with a darning plate to cover the feed dogs and prevent them from moving. It's a good idea to practise on a piece of fabric you're not too precious about. It may help to use a stabiliser on the back of your fabric.

Key techniques

Snipping into curves

Cutting small 'V' shapes into the seam allowance of curves will help to reduce bulk and allow the seam to sit flat without puckering. Pinking shears are useful tools for speedy snipping, or a sharp pair of scissors will do the trick!

Cutting corners

To reduce bulk and create sharper points, cut across the corners of a project that will be turned through, but be careful not to cut through the stitches.

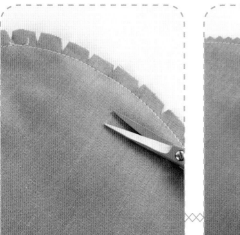

VIDEOS

Cutting and folding bias binding

Continuous bias binding

Bias binding

I use quite a lot of bias binding in my projects as it's a simple way to finish off raw edges and it gives a professional finish. Although it can be bought in many colours and widths, I like to make my own as it's not only cost-effective, it also means I can coordinate my fabrics. Bias tape is so called because it is a strip of fabric cut at a 45-degree angle along the bias of the fabric. This allows a little 'give', so that the fabric can stretch around curves without puckering. To cut your fabric accurately you'll need a rotary cutter, rectangular ruler and cutting mat.

1 Lay your fabric squarely on the cutting mat and, using the 45 degree mark, place the ruler on the straight edge of the fabric. And cut! Use the straight side of the ruler to measure the width you need. For 2.5cm (1in) tape you'll need to cut 5cm (2in) of fabric. As you're cutting the strips, your cut line will become longer, so fold the fabric in half, matching up the diagonal edges, and cut through two, three or four layers at a time.

2 To join the strips together, lay two pieces right sides together, overlapping at right angles. Draw a diagonal line from one corner to the other across the overlap. Pin, then sew across this line. Trim the raw edge back to around 3mm (1/8in) and press the seam open.

3 Making bias binding involves folding over both the long edges into the centre and pressing. The easiest way to do this is to use a small bias tape maker, through which you thread the tape. It folds the strip in two and you press with your iron while pulling the fabric through. If you don't have a tape maker, carefully fold both long edges to the centre of the fabric strip and press. Be careful not to get your fingers too close to the iron!

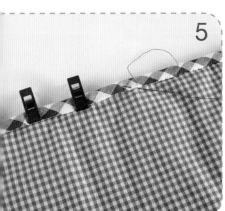

4 To apply the binding, open up the crease lines and, right sides together, pin across the raw edge of your work. Sew with your machine along the upper crease mark.

5 Fold the tape over the raw edge, and use slip stitch to sew by hand.

Tip

If you're applying the bias tape continuously, start by opening up the creases and folding over the end of the tape; then pin and machine sew as in step 4. When you get back to the start, overlap the ends of the tape by about 5mm (1/4in). Fold over and stitch as in step 5. Instead of slip stitching by hand you could machine topstitch.

MITRING A CORNER

If the bias binding is attached around a curve it will stretch easily, but if you want to mitre a corner, this is how to do it.

VIDEO

Applying bias binding

1 Sew along the upper crease line but stop 5mm (¼in) from the corner and back-tack to stop the stitches from coming undone. Fold the tape along the second side, making a triangular pleat in the corner. Fold the pleat away from your stitch line, and sew straight down the second side.

2 Open up the tape at the corner and you should see a neat mitre forming. As you fold the tape over, mirror the same mitre on the reverse. Secure the back of the tape with slip stitch.

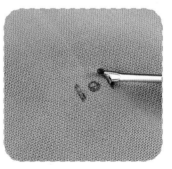

Applying magnetic clasps

Although they are a simple way to add closures to projects, magnetic clasps don't generally come with instructions, so this may help!

1 Your clasp will be in two halves – one thin and one thick. If applying to a bag with a flap, the thicker part will go on the bag and the thinner on the flap. Mark the position of the clasp by drawing through the backing disc.

2 Make small cuts either side of the centre spot, either with your quick unpick or a small, sharp pair of scissors. Start small – you can always make a small hole bigger, but if you make the cuts too big you'll just have holes in your fabric!

3 Push the prongs of the clasp through the slits and then the backing disc.

4 Open out the prongs on the back of the fabric. It's a good idea to place a square of fabric behind the clasp to help strengthen the closure, particularly on fine fabrics.

Knotted Headband

So simple and quick to make, this pretty headband is the perfect finishing touch for the well-dressed baby!

Finished size

66 x 5cm (26 x 2in)

What you need

Two strips of contrasting fabric, each measuring 67 x 6cm (26½ x 2½in)

4cm (1½in) circular template: I used a ribbon reel

Marking pen

1 Measure 6.5cm (2½in) from the ends of each piece of fabric and draw a semicircle on each side using your template. Cut the curve from either side of the strip. Trim the ends of the fabric into curves too.

2 Sew the two strips right sides together, leaving a turning gap of about 7.5cm (3in) in one side. Snip into the curves and turn right side out. Press, then topstitch around the edge.

3 Wrap around baby's head and knot as you like.

Tip
To get the perfect fit, measure around baby's head, then add 12.75cm (5in).

Hooded Towel

How lovely and snuggly to be wrapped in this foxy-faced towel after bathtime! The fleecy outside makes it extra cosy and soft. Use a 1cm (½in) seam allowance.

Finished size

73.5cm (29in) square

What you need

76.25 x 101.5cm (30 x 40in) white towelling fabric

76.25cm (30in) square printed fleece fabric

44.5 x 35cm (17½ x 14in) plain brown fleece

Two button eyes: I used googly eye buttons

Pompom for the nose

1 Cut a 76.25cm (30in) square from the towelling fabric. Both towelling and fleece fabrics tend to shed a lot, so be prepared to get covered in fluff! Cut a curve from one top corner of both the towelling and fleece squares.

2 Use the curved corner as a template to cut one piece from towelling and one from plain fleece, measuring 44.5cm (17½in) across the bottom and 20.5cm (8in) high. These will form the fox's head.

3 Sew the two pieces right sides together across the straight side, then fold so that the wrong sides are together. Topstitch along the seam.

4 For the ears, draw a triangle measuring 10cm (4in) across the bottom and 12.75cm (5in) tall, then curve the long sides. Cut out four pieces the same.

5 Sew the ear pieces right sides together in pairs, leaving the bottom (straight) edges open. Turn right side out.

6 Pin, then tack/baste the ears facing inwards right sides together to the sides of the plain fleece. Remove the pins.

7 Place this head piece back over the curved corner of the fleece square, right sides together. Pin the towelling square over the top so that the head is sandwiched in between the two pieces and the curved corners match up. Sew all the way round, leaving a turning gap in one side of about 10cm (4in). Turn right side out and topstitch all the way round. Sew on your button eyes securely, then add the pompom nose to the front of the hood.

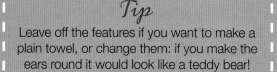

Tip
Leave off the features if you want to make a plain towel, or change them: if you make the ears round it would look like a teddy bear!

Play Mat

Engage baby's senses with this fun, colourful play mat with stimulating rattles, squeakers and textures. Add more texture with faux fur, corduroy, laminates and any other fabrics you have in your stash! I've used a strong fabric glue to fix on the ribbons, flowers and button before sewing because we need all these pieces to be secure so that little hands cannot pull them off. Never leave baby unattended.

Finished size

51 x 79cm (20 x 31in)

What you need

53.5 x 81.25cm (21 x 32in) top fabric

53.5 x 81.25cm (21 x 32in) bottom fabric (I used the same fabric as the top)

Four squares of brightly coloured fabric, each measuring approximately 30.5cm (12in)

Two squares of natural felt – in different colours – measuring approximately 23cm (9in)

15.25cm (6in) square of green fleece for the leaves

One button

Seven strips of ribbon each measuring 102cm (40in) long, three 1cm (½in) wide and four 5mm (¼in) wide

33 x 51cm (13 x 20in) sew-in interfacing

Embroidery thread

51 x 79cm (20 x 31in) of 1cm (½in) thick polyester wadding/batting (you could use foam)

25.5cm (10in) square of heat-reflective foam

7.5cm (3in), 20.5cm (8in), 23cm (9in) and 30.5cm (12in) circle templates

Erasable ink pen

Strong wet fabric glue

A collection of rattles, squeakers and crinkly plastic sheets

Temporary glue pen

Small amount of toy filler

1 Cut a 23cm (9in) circle of heat-reflective foam using your circle template.

2 Using your 30.5cm (12in) template, round the corners of the top and bottom fabrics, and do the same with the wadding/batting.

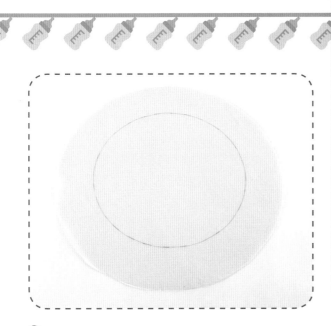

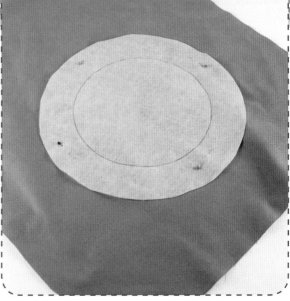

3 Cut a 30.5cm (12in) circle of sew-in interfacing, then draw a 20.5cm (8in) circle in the centre.

4 Pin centrally to the right side of the top fabric, 10cm (4in) from one end. Sew around the inner circle.

5 Remove the pins, then cut out the inner circle with a 3mm ($\frac{1}{8}$in) seam allowance. Push the interfacing through the hole and press.

6 Place the heat-reflective foam under the hole and secure with your temporary glue pen, then sew in place with a long stitch on your machine.

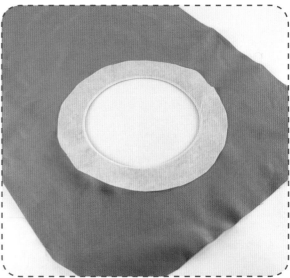

7 Cut six 7.5cm (3in) circles of fabric, two each of three colours. Sew each circle to a piece of interfacing, right sides facing, with a 3mm ($^1/_8$in) seam allowance. Cut a slit into the interfacing, then turn each circle right side out and press. These will form your flower centres.

8 Cut out twenty petal shapes using the template on page 95 – these will form ten petals, five each for two of the flowers. Sew together in pairs leaving the straight side open. Trim around the curved edge with pinking shears.

9 Turn right side out and press. Pop a little toy filler into the petal, along with a rattle or squeaker.

10 Put a spot of glue in the open end of the petal and secure with a pin or clip until dry.

11 Add a little toy filler to the centre of the two flower centres (created in step 7). Glue five of the petals in place behind each fabric circle.

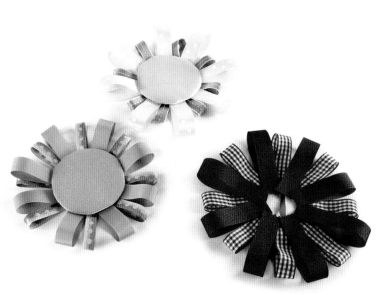

12 For each of the three ribbon flowers, cut sixteen 12.75cm (5in) strips of ribbon, eight each of two different types. Fold the strips in half and glue, then glue evenly around the back of the lined fabric circles. Add a little toy filler to the centres.

13 Use the petal template to cut five petal shapes from felt to make another flower. Add a little toy filler to the centre circle, then glue the felt petals in place on the back of it.

14 Arrange your flowers on the play mat. Cut out a couple of leaf shapes from fleece and satin stitch them in place. When you're happy with the arrangement, tie a 20.5cm (8in) piece of ribbon to each of your rattles, glue, place the ribbon end under the flowers, then sew around the centre of each flower to secure.

15 To make the butterfly, cut out four large and four small wings, plus two pieces of crinkly plastic from the large wing pattern (see page 95). Place the large wing pieces together in pairs, right sides facing, then place a piece of plastic over a wrong side of each pair. Sew these three layers together with a 3mm (1/8in) seam allowance, leaving the straight side open. Turn right side out. Pinch a small pleat in the centre of each large wing and tack/baste. Sew the smaller wings together in the same way but don't pleat these.

16 Cut two butterfly body pieces from felt. Embroider a little face onto one side. Sandwich the wings in between the two body pieces, add a 41cm (16in) length of ribbon to the bottom, and secure with a few spots of glue. When the glue is dry, topstitch around the body.

17 Glue the end of the butterfly ribbon to the centre of one of the flowers, then hand sew a button over the top.

18 Place the top of the play mat over the wadding/batting. Pin the backing fabric right sides together over the top, making sure that all the attachments are tucked inside away from the edge. Sew all the way around with a 1cm (½in) seam allowance, leaving a turning gap of about 15.25cm (6in). Turn right side out and press, then hand sew the opening closed. Topstitch all around the mat, approximately 2cm (¾in) from the edge.

Tip
Try not to bend the reflective foam too much – it will crease easily.

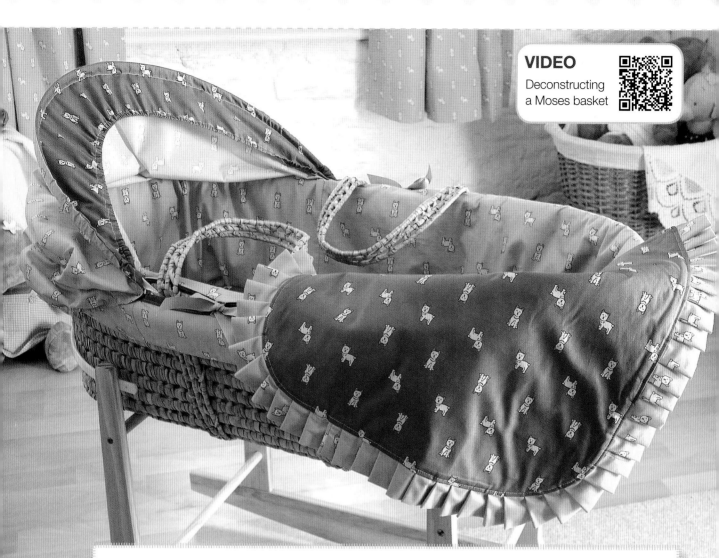

VIDEO
Deconstructing
a Moses basket

Finished size

My basket measures 84 x 43 x 25.5cm
(33 x 17 x 10in) – yours may be different

What you need

Moses basket with cover, hood and mattress

For the cover:
102 x 183cm (40 x 72in) fabric
142.25cm (56in) of 5mm (¼in) wide elastic
114.5cm (45in) of 2.5cm (1in) wide bias binding
81.5cm (32in) of 1cm (½in) wide ribbon

For the hood:
91.5 x 66cm (36 x 26in) yellow fabric
91.5 x 15.25cm (36 x 6in) grey fabric for the
front panel
152.5cm (60in) of 5mm (¼in) wide elastic

For the coverlet:
45.75 x 48.25cm (18 x 19in) top fabric
45.75 x 48.25cm (18 x 19in) bottom fabric
45.75 x 48.25cm (18 x 19in) wadding/batting
For the frill, 30.5 x 137cm (12 x 54in) fabric cut
into 10cm (4in) wide strips

For the mattress:
102 x 76cm (40 x 30in) fabric

Moses Basket

Baby's first bed will probably be a Moses basket and there are some beautiful designs on the market. However, designer brands can be very expensive, and if you have a specific fabric colour or theme in mind it can be difficult to find exactly what you want. The easiest and most affordable way of making a bespoke basket is to buy a cheaper model, then use the cover as a template to create your own unique bedding.

I've listed the materials for the cover, hood and coverlet separately in case you don't wish to make them all. My basket measures 84 x 43 x 25.5cm (33 x 17 x 10in) – you'll find it easier to cover if you choose a plain cover with no ruffles or frills. Use a 1cm (½in) seam allowance.

Tip
Your basket may be made differently to mine, so make note of how it is constructed. Take photographs of your basket before deconstructing the cover, just in case you forget how the pieces fit together. See also the video, left, for advice on a different construction method.

1 Remove the covers. You may find it useful to write the position on each section, such as base, sides and hood, for example, to identify the pieces. The elastic will probably be sewn into the seams so it's easier to cut it off completely. Cut along the seams to separate each panel. Use these panels as templates to cut your fabric; as you've cut the seams off the original cover, add 1cm (½in) seam allowance all around each piece. For my cover, I have two end pieces measuring 84 x 38cm (33 x 15in), two bottom side panels measuring 28 x 25.5cm (11 x 10in) and two top side pieces measuring 28 x 12.75cm (11 x 5in). The base of my cover is 84 x 35.5cm (33 x 14in) with rounded corners. I'm reusing the existing padding.

2 Place each set of side panels together as shown – the gap between them will fit over the basket handles. Cut the ribbon into four and tack/baste, facing inwards, to each side of the opening.

3 Fold the bias binding in half lengthways and press. Fold it over the raw edges of the openings and sew; fold the ribbon over the bias binding as you sew to trap it so that it sits facing over the top.

4 Sew the ends and sides of the cover right sides together to make a large 'loop' of fabric.

5 Pin, then sew the loop onto the base, right sides together, with the handle openings at the sides. The easiest way to do this is to fold the base into four and crease the centre of each side, then repeat with the sides of the cover and line up the crease marks. If the fit isn't exact you may have to make a few small pleats – keep these in the corners and they will look deliberate. Also bear in mind that the mattress will cover the seam. Remove the pins.

6 Fold over the hem by 5mm (¼in) twice, then sew a length of elastic to the inside of the cover with a triple zigzag stitch if you have one on your machine, or a wide zigzag stitch if not, stretching the elastic as you sew.

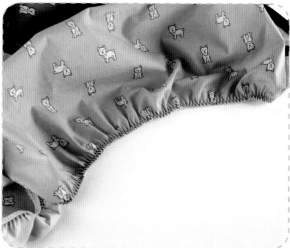

7 Fit the cover over the basket, threading the handles through the slits, then tie the ribbons to secure.

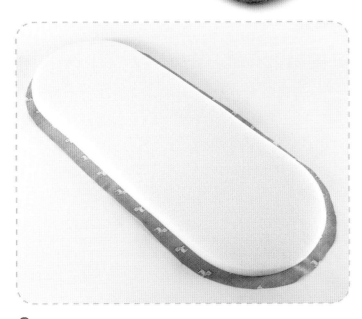

8 Use the mattress as a template to cut one piece of fabric, 2.5cm (1in) larger all the way round – this is the front.

9 Measure two thirds from one curved end of the fabric, then cut two pieces of fabric to this shape – these will overlap to form the envelope opening on the back. Fold over the straight sides twice by 5mm (¼in) each time and topstitch.

10 Starting at the curved sides, pin the two back pieces to the front, right sides together – the back pieces should overlap. Sew all the way round then remove the pins. Snip around the curves, turn right side out and press. Insert the mattress pad.

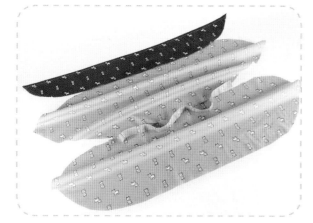

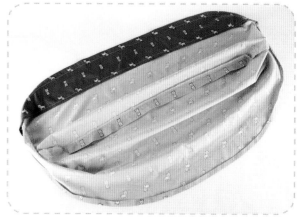

11 Remove the bars from your hood, then cut apart the fabric panels, removing any elastic and unpicking the hems. Mine has two large pieces with a tubular channel that fits in between the two, and an elasticated front panel. Use these pieces as templates to cut the shapes from your new fabric. Hem the front panel along the long straight edge (I used grey fabric here) by folding the fabric over twice and topstitching. Hem the short ends of the tubular channel in the same way, then fold in half lengthways and press.

12 Sew the two large pieces right sides together along the centre seam. Place the folded tube along the seam centrally, on the wrong side of the hood, and sew it onto the seam allowance.

13 Sew the front panel right sides together to the top of the hood. Hem the remaining raw edge around the whole piece. Fold the front (grey) panel over the hood, wrong sides together, and sew a line 2.5cm (1in) from the seam, attaching the front and main piece together to create a channel, leaving the ends open at each end to fit one of the hood bars. To neaten the seams on the inside of the hood, sew overedge stitch along all the edges – if you don't have this stitch on your sewing machine, use zigzag stitch.

14 Using triple zigzag stitch, sew elastic all the way around the hem, making sure you leave a gap at each end of the channel to feed the tube through. Your hood is now ready to be fitted! Push one hood bar through the top channel, and one through the tubular channel, then fix to each side of your basket.

15 As I bought an inexpensive basket, the coverlet was filled with polyester wadding/batting so I've replaced it with more breathable wool. Use the original coverlet as a template to cut two pieces of fabric 1cm (½in) bigger all the way round.

16 Cut the new wadding/batting to the same size as the coverlet. I'm adding a pleated frill – the strip of fabric to make this measures three times the length of the sides and bottom edge of the coverlet by 10cm (4in) in width. You may need to join a few strips. Press the strip in half lengthways, fold under the two short ends and sew. Pinch into 1cm (½in) pleats and pin.

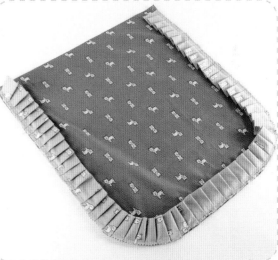

17 Pin the frill in place around the curved edge of the top fabric, aligning the raw edges and with the frill facing inwards. Sew along the raw edge of the pleats to secure them, starting and finishing 1cm (½in) from the top straight edge. Snip into the curves with pinking shears.

18 Place the back of the blanket cover right sides together with the frilled side, lay the wadding/batting on top and pin. Sew all the way around, leaving a turning gap of about 10cm (4in) in one side. Make sure you don't include the end of the frill in the seam. Snip around the curves and corners. Turn right side out and press. Topstitch all the way round.

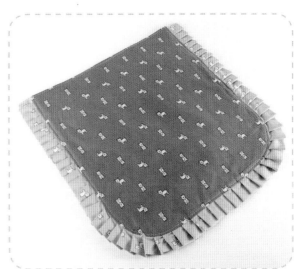

Balloon Mobile

This fun mobile will brighten up the nursery and delight the youngsters! Try hanging a string of balloons across a window to create a matching garland.

Finished size

Including hanging cord, 25.5 x 86.5cm (10 x 34in)

What you need

One plain and two patterned fabrics, 38cm (15in) square of each

Scraps of felt in assorted colours for the bunting

250g (9oz) toy filler

Embroidery thread in four colours, including black

Embroidery needle

Clear thread

About 214cm (84in) of 1cm (½in) wide ribbon

About 75 buttons

20.5cm (8in) wooden embroidery hoop

127cm (50in) cord for hanging

Strong fabric glue

Erasable ink pen

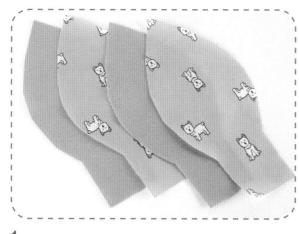

1 Cut out four pattern pieces for each balloon, two each of two fabrics (see template on page 95).

2 For each balloon, sew the four pieces right sides together, leaving the short, straight ends unsewn and alternating the fabric patterns.

3 Turn right side out. Fold the raw edge over twice and sew, then stuff with toy filler.

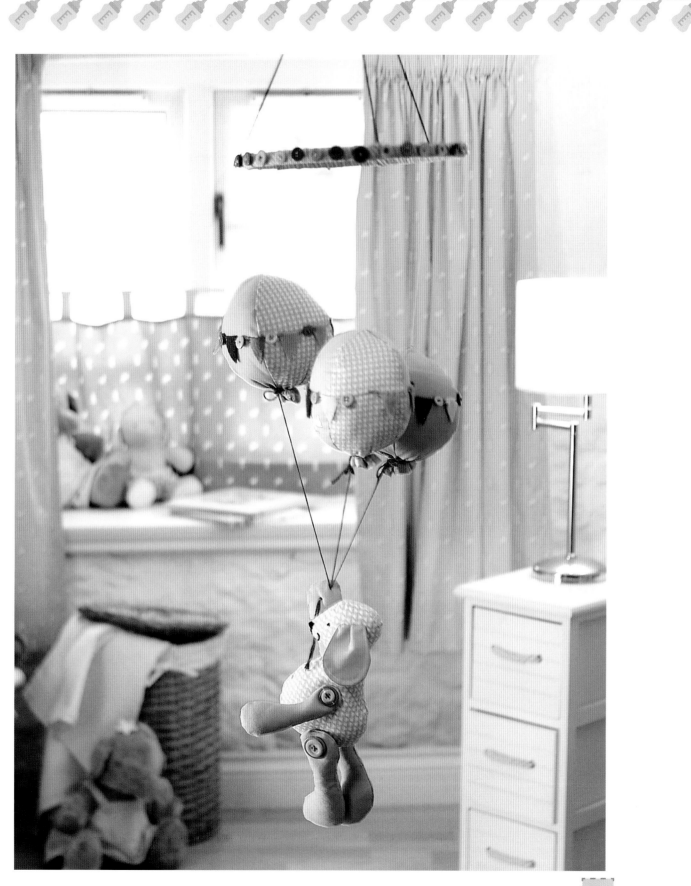

4 Make a running stitch by hand around the base of the ball shape and pull to gather.

5 Cut out thirty triangles from felt using your template (see page 95). Take a length of embroidery thread (six strands) and sew ten triangles and ten buttons alternately onto the thread. Repeat twice more, using different coloured threads.

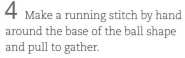

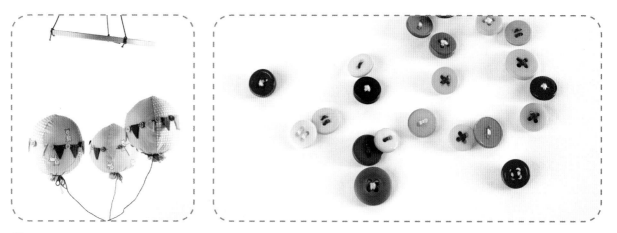

6 Wrap each garland around a balloon and knot, then secure with fabric glue. Sew a 25.5cm (10in) length of clear thread to the top of each balloon. Tie a 38cm (15in) length of embroidery thread to the bottom of each balloon. Divide the embroidery hoop into thirds and mark. Tie the balloons to the hoop, staggering the lengths of the clear thread slightly. Cut three 25.5cm (10in) lengths of cord and tie to the hoop; knot together. Knot the hanging embroidery thread lengths together approximately 10cm (4in) from the ends.

7 Take 45 of the buttons and sew embroidery thread through the holes. These will be glued onto the hoop, but the thread makes them look as if they've been sewn on! Wrap the ribbon around the hoop – secure the ends of the ribbon with a dot of glue. Glue the buttons over the ribbon.

8 Cut out two dog body pattern pieces (see page 94). Sew the body sections right sides together, leaving a turning gap in the back of about 5cm (2in). Turn right side out and stuff with toy filler, then hand sew the opening closed.

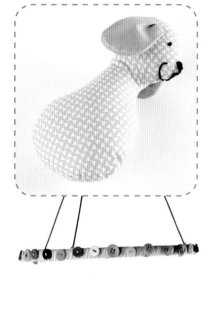

9 Cut four ear pieces (see page 94). Sew them right sides together in pairs leaving the top open, snip around the curve then turn right side out. Fold the open ends inwards and press. Topstitch around the curved sides.

10 Cut four arm pieces and four leg pieces. Sew the pieces right sides together in pairs, leaving a turning gap in one side of about 4cm (1½in). Turn right side out and stuff with toy filler; hand sew the openings closed.

11 Pinch the tops of the ears to make small pleats, then hand sew evenly to either side of the head. Draw the position of the eyes, nose and mouth with your erasable ink pen and embroider with black thread.

12 Attach the arms and legs by sewing straight through the body, adding a couple of buttons on each side.

13 Sew the ends of the balloon ties through one of the dog's paws, and knot.

Chair Harness

When visiting friends or dining out and a high chair isn't available, this chair harness will really come in handy! It's easy to adapt in length if you have a specific chair in mind. Never leave baby unattended.

1 Fold the 10 x 28cm (4 x 11in) strips of fabric in half lengthways and press. Unfold, then fold the long edges to the centre and press, fold in half completely and press again. Topstitch along the two long sides.

Finished size

45.75 x 114.5cm (18 x 45in)

What you need

In total, 112 x 152.5cm (44 x 60in) fabric

81.25 x 91.5cm (32 x 36in) wadding/batting

3.65m (4yd) of 2.5cm (1in) wide bias binding

Fabric marking pen

Repositionable spray fabric adhesive

51cm (20in) of 3mm ($^1/_8$in) wide elastic

Bodkin or safety pin

Cut

Cut two pieces of fabric and one of wadding/ batting measuring 28 x 35.5cm (11 x 14in)
Cut two pieces of fabric and one of wadding/ batting measuring 28 x 56cm (11 x 22in)
Cut two pieces of fabric and one of wadding/ batting measuring 53.5 x 35.5cm (21 x 14in)
Cut two pieces of fabric measuring 10 x 28cm (4 x 11in)
Cut two pieces of fabric measuring 10 x 91.5cm (4 x 36in)

2 Sew together the two 10 x 91.5cm (4 x 36in) strips of fabric to create one long strip, then fold and press as above, but this time turn the ends in by 1cm (½in) first to make neat.

3 Adhere the corresponding wadding/batting to the wrong side of one piece of each fabric. Take the two 53.5 x 35.5cm (21 x 14in) pieces of fabric, measure and mark 20.5cm (8in) from one bottom corner up one short side and 20.5cm (8in) along the long bottom edge. Draw a curve from the side mark to the bottom mark. Fold the fabric in half and cut out the curve – this is to make the shape symmetrical.

4 Take the two fabric pieces measuring 28 x 56cm (11 x 22in). Measure and mark 7.5cm (3in) from one bottom corner up one long side and 7.5cm (3in) along the short bottom edge. Draw a curve from the side mark to the bottom, fold in half and cut.

5 Sew the 28cm (11in) straps to the 28 x 35.5cm (11 x 14in) piece of fabric backed with wadding/ batting, 7.5cm (3in) from either side. Remove the pins. Then sew across the straps 7.5cm (3in) from the top and 7.5cm (3in) from the bottom.

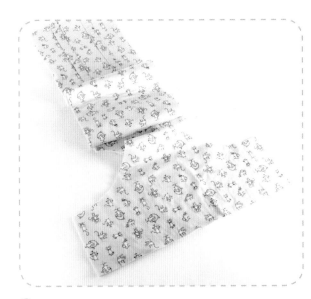

6 Sew the top of the padded section with the straps to the uncut top of the long padded piece created in step 4, right sides together. Sew the bottom of each cut-out padded section right sides together, to make one long strip. Sew together the remaining, unpadded fabric pieces in the same way.

7 Pin the two pieces wrong sides together and tack/ baste all the way round, 3mm (¹/₈in) from the edge. You could use spray adhesive here if you wish. Sew across the seams.

8 Apply bias binding to the cut-out curved sections.

9 Cut the elastic in half. Using your bodkin or safety pin, thread a piece of elastic through the bias tape, pull slightly, then sew each end of the elastic to the bias tape.

10 Add bias binding around the remaining raw edges. Fold over the front of the harness by 5cm (2in) and sew, leaving the ends open to make a channel. Thread the long strap through this channel.

11 Slip the cover over the chair back, sit baby on the seat and tie the strap securely around the back, through the straps.

Bandana Bib

Made from the softest brushed cotton, this stylish bib not only adds the finishing touch to baby's outfit, it helps to keep it clean, too!

Finished size

35.5 x 14cm (14 x 5½in)

What you need

41 x 18cm (16 x 7in) brushed cotton

41 x 18cm (16 x 7in) fleece or towelling

Card, pen and ruler to make a template

One plastic snap fastener

1 Draw a triangle shape on your card measuring 38cm (15in) across the top and 15.25cm (6in) deep. Draw a gentle curve on the outside of one short side, and the inside of the long side.

2 Fold the template in half to make it symmetrical and cut around the curved lines. Cut one shape from brushed cotton and one from fleece.

Tip

Add a 10cm (4in) strip of ribbon with a plastic snap fastener on the end to the point of the bib to secure a dummy/pacifier!

3 Sew the two fabric pieces right sides together, leaving a turning gap of about 7.5cm (3in). Snip across the points, turn right side out and press; fold the edges of the turning gap inwards.

4 Topstitch around the edge. Attach one half of the plastic snap fastener to each end of the long side following the manufacturer's instructions.

5 The bandana simply fastens around baby's neck.

Baby Nest

Baby nests are becoming increasingly popular for newborns to babies of about three months, but they can be quite expensive to buy. Making your own is so much more cost-effective and means your nest will match the decor in your nursery! Make up a few sheets to help protect the bottom of the nest.

VIDEO

Making a baby nest

Finished size

76.25 x 51 x 12.75cm (30 x 20 x 5in)

What you need

For the nest:

66 x 30.5cm (26 x 12in) of 1cm (½in) deep foam for the base

30.5cm (12in) circle template

66 x 99cm (26 x 39in) outer fabric

66 x 99cm (26 x 39in) inner fabric

4 x 285cm (1½ x 112in) strip of bias-cut fabric to make the ribbon channel

10 x 285cm (4 x 112in) strip of bias-cut fabric for the frill

2.75m (3yd) of 3mm (⅛in) wide ribbon

Ruler and erasable marking pen

500g (17½oz) toy filler

Safety pin or bodkin

For the sheet:

One piece of cotton fabric measuring 71 x 35.5cm (28 x 14in)

One piece of towelling fabric measuring 71 x 35.5cm (28 x 14in)

Card and pencil to make a template

1 Use the circle template to round off the short ends of the foam. Make a template from this shape to make the sheet.

2 Place the foam in the centre of the outer piece of fabric and measure and mark 15.25cm (6in) around all sides. Cut out this new shape, then use this as a template to cut the inner piece of fabric to the same shape. Draw around the foam with an erasable ink pen on the right side of one piece of fabric to mark its position in the centre.

3 Fold the strips of frill and channel fabrics in half lengthways and press. Open out the frill fabric, fold one short end of the frill under by 1cm (½in), and press again. Refold the fabric, then sew the frill facing inwards to the right side of the base fabric, starting 2.5cm (1in) from the end. When you come back to the start, slip the raw end inside the folded end to make neat. To make the channel, open out one end of the fabric and press it in by 1cm (½in). Refold, then sew on top of the frill, starting in the centre of one curved end. When the ends meet, stop sewing a couple of inches before, open out the end of the fabric and fold inwards, so that when you continue sewing, the two folded ends of the channel meet, as shown.

4 Pin the inner fabric right sides together to the outer and sew around the edge, leaving a gap of about 15.25cm (6in) in each long side.

5 Turn right side out. Making sure the two pieces are lying flat, sew around one half of the oval mark in the centre of the nest. Slip the foam inside, then continue sewing.

6 Stuff toy filler through both side gaps, then hand stitch the openings closed.

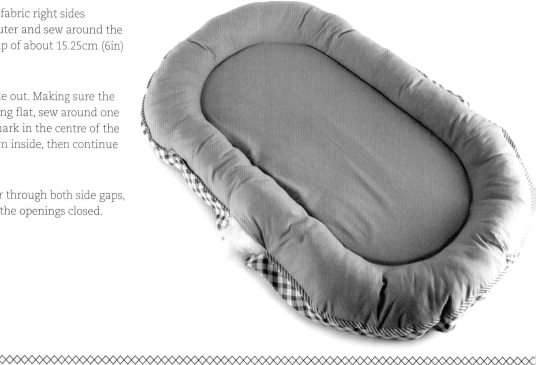

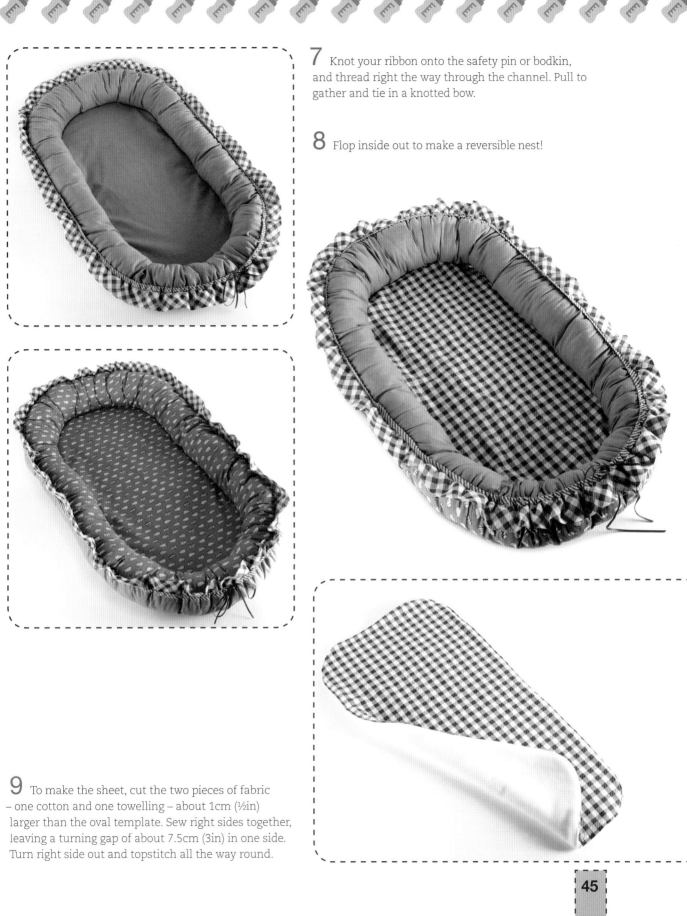

7 Knot your ribbon onto the safety pin or bodkin, and thread right the way through the channel. Pull to gather and tie in a knotted bow.

8 Flop inside out to make a reversible nest!

9 To make the sheet, cut the two pieces of fabric – one cotton and one towelling – about 1cm (½in) larger than the oval template. Sew right sides together, leaving a turning gap of about 7.5cm (3in) in one side. Turn right side out and topstitch all the way round.

Cot Bumper

VIDEO
Piping

This protective padded bumper coordinates perfectly with your cot quilt (see page 88), and is made to measure, so will fit your cot perfectly.

see page 88

1 Make a template of the end of your cot by pushing the card or paper into the shape of the cot and creasing it into the corners. Fold the card in half and cut out the shape of the cot end so that it is symmetrical. Cut a gentle curve around the top of the template. Before cutting your fabric, reinsert the card into the end of the cot to make sure it fits perfectly.

Finished size

For my cot, the centre measures 63.5 x 61cm (25 x 24in); the sides are 67.5 x 29.25cm (26½ x 11½in) each

What you need

For the patchwork, four coordinating fat quarters

For the plain bumper top, about 63.5 x 25.5cm (25 x 10in) fabric

1.25m (1¼yd) backing fabric

3.75m (4yd) of 5mm (¼in) piping cord

3.75m (4yd) of 2.5cm (1in) wide bias tape for the piping

1.5m (1½yd) of 2.5cm (1in) bias binding: mine is the same fabric as the piping tape

203 x 56cm (80 x 22in) premium quilt wadding/batting

4.5m (5yd) of 1cm (½in) wide ribbon cut into ten equal strips

Large piece of card or paper to make a template

2 Cut your fat quarters into 11cm (4¼in) squares. Sew seven squares together, with right sides facing, to form a strip of squares. Repeat three more times. Then sew the rows together, until you have an area that will cover about three-quarters of the height of the template (you may need more or fewer squares, depending on the size of your cot). Trim the top of the patchwork section to the same curve as the top of your template.

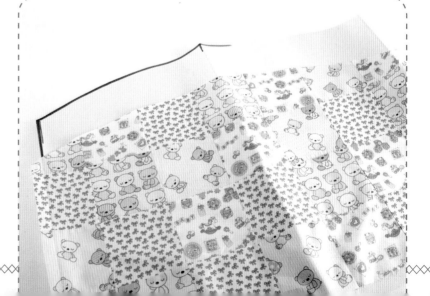

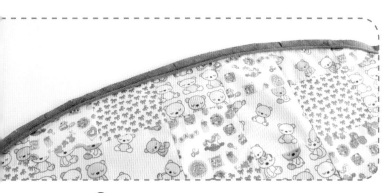

3 Make the piping by folding the 2.5cm (1in) bias tape around the cord, wrong sides facing, and sew along the edge of the cord with the zipper foot on your machine. Trim the seam allowance to 5mm (¼in). Sew a piece of this piping cord to the curved top of the patchwork piece, raw edges together. Snip into the seam allowance.

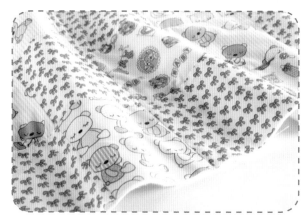

4 Fold the raw edge of the piping to the back of the patchwork and press, so that the piping sits on top of the fabric. Place this piece over the plain fabric, leaving about 20.5cm (8in) from the top of the curve to the top of the plain fabric. Pin, then sew along the piping seam to attach. Remove the pins.

5 Cut the top of the plain section to the same shape as the patchwork, creating a 15.25cm (6in) plain border at the top. Pin this whole section onto a piece of wadding/batting. Sew along the seams – 'stitch in the ditch' – to quilt. Trim away any excess wadding/batting.

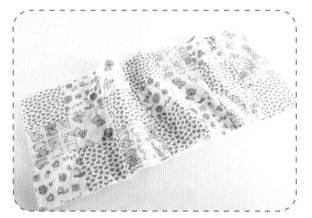

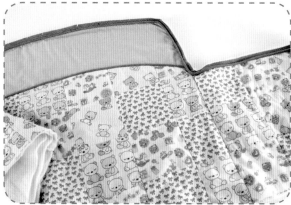

6 To make each of the two side panels, sew together patchworked squares that are three squares deep and seven squares across. Place on top of wadding/batting and quilt by stitching in the ditch.

7 Sew these side panel pieces right sides together to each side of the cot head panel, matching up the seams. Apply piping around the top and sides, as you did in step 3.

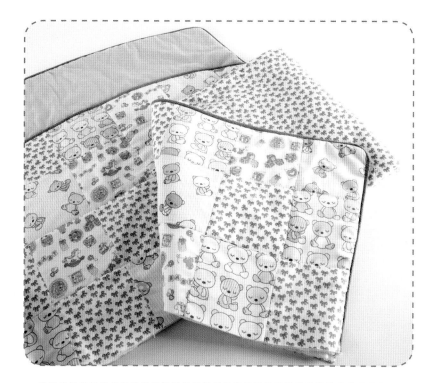

8 Use this whole piece as a template to cut your backing fabric. Sew the two pieces right sides together around the top and sides, clip into the curves and corners, turn right side out and press.

9 Sew a strip of bias binding across the bottom of the bumper – fold the ends of the binding inwards to make neat. Position the bumper in the cot and mark where the ribbon ties will fit best. Remove the bumper, fold the ribbon strips in half and sew in place. I've sewn two to the top, three along each side seam then two on each end.

Cot Pocket

Keep essentials to hand with this useful pocket
that simply hangs over the side of your cot.

Finished size

Including straps, 25.5 x 31.75cm (10 x 12½in)

What you need

56 x 28cm (22 x 11in) fabric
57 x 36cm (22½ x 14in) pocket fabric
38cm (15in) of 2.5cm (1in) wide bias binding
37 x 45.75cm (14½ x 18in) wadding/batting
Three buttons

1 Cut two pieces of backing fabric and one of wadding/batting measuring 27cm (10½in) square. For the pocket, cut two pieces of pocket fabric and one piece of wadding/batting measuring 37 x 18cm (14½ x 7in). The straps are two strips of pocket fabric measuring 10 x 20.5cm (4 x 8in). Fold the straps in half lengthways and press. Fold the raw edges to the centre then in half again, to make two strips measuring 2.5 x 20.5cm (1 x 8in). Fold one end inwards by 1cm (½in) and press again, then topstitch around the three folded sides.

2 Sew a buttonhole across the hemmed end of each strap to fit your buttons. I find it easier to position the buttonhole if I stitch one out on a scrap piece of fabric first.

3 Place the pocket pieces wrong sides together with the corresponding wadding/batting sandwiched in the centre. Sew the bias binding across the top (see page 12).

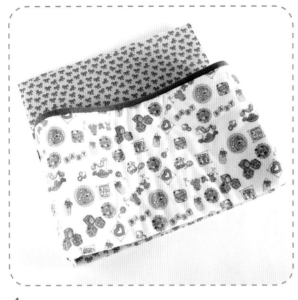

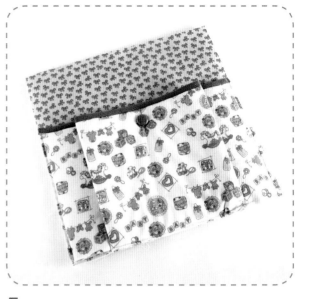

4 Place one square of fabric over the wadding/batting square. Pin the pocket on top, aligning the bottom edges, and sew the sides of the pocket to the sides of the square, close to the edge.

5 Form two equal pleats, 5cm (2in) from each side, then sew across the bottom of the pocket, again, close to the edge. Hand sew one of the buttons to the centre of the pocket to divide it, through all layers of fabric, 2.5cm (1in) from the top.

6 Tack/baste the straps, facing inwards, 5cm (2in) from either side of the square, along the top – ensure the buttonholed ends are away from the seam (see the tip, opposite).

7 Sew the remaining two buttons under the straps, 2cm (¾in) from the top, as shown.

8 Fold the straps back down and place the remaining fabric square on top of the whole piece. Sew together all round, leaving a turning gap of about 7.5cm (3in) in one side. Snip across the corners, turn right side out and press. Topstitch around the edge.

9 Button up over the side of your cot.

Tip
Measure the distance of the bars on your cot to make sure the straps are positioned in the right place.

Insulated Bottle Bag

Keep baby's drinks warmer (or cooler!) for longer with this handy insulated bag, ideal for picnics and days out! My bottle measures 19cm (7½in) tall.

Finished size

Not including strap, 7.5 x 7.5 x 24cm (3 x 3 x 9½in)

What you need

25.5 x 23cm (10 x 9in) lower (star) fabric
25.5 x 18cm (10 x 7in) top (check) fabric
5 x 51cm (2 x 20in) fabric for the strap
25.5 x 40.5cm (10 x 16in) insulated wadding/batting
25.5 x 40.5cm (10 x 16in) heat-reflective fabric
Repositionable spray fabric adhesive
Four decorative buttons
One hook-and-loop dot (both parts)

1 Fold the long sides of the strap fabric to the centre and press. Unfold, then fold the long edges to the centre and press. Fold in half again and press. Sew along the two long sides.

54

2 Measure and mark 7.5cm (3in) from each side of the top (longer edge) of the lower (star) fabric, tack/baste the strap over these marks, making sure the strap isn't twisted. Sew the top and lower fabrics right sides together, sandwiching the strap in between. Topstitch along each side of the seam.

3 Take the insulated wadding/batting and cut a rectangle from each top corner of the shorter edge, 7.5cm (3in) across the top and 10cm (4in) deep. Use the wadding/batting as a template to cut the same shape from the outer and reflective fabrics.

4 Fuse the wadding/batting to the wrong side of the outer fabric with a little repositionable spray adhesive. Sew the top of the outer and reflective pieces right sides together around the cut-out corners and the top, snip off the corners and cut into the inverted corners.

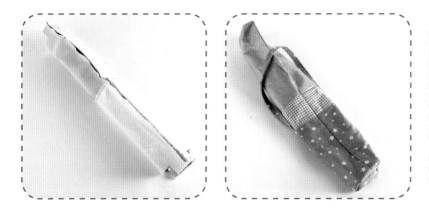

5 Fold the bag in half, right sides together – lining to lining and outer to outer – so that the long edges meet, and sew; leave a turning gap of about 10cm (4in) in the lining. Roll flat so that the seam is in the centre, then cut a 2.5cm (1in) square from each corner, as shown.

6 Sew across each end of the tube. Open out the cut-out corners, aligning the seams, and sew across to make the base of the bag square. Turn right side out and sew the turning gap closed.

7 Push the lining inside the bag. Hand sew the hook-and-loop dots to the underside of the flap and over the seam of the bag to correspond, then add three buttons over the seam and one on the flap to decorate. Pop in your bottle and enjoy your day out!

Patchwork Pillow

When reading or singing to baby, relax in stylish comfort with this pretty patchwork pillow!

Finished size

41 x 41cm (16 x 16in)

What you need

For a 41cm (16in) square pillow you will need:

33cm (13in) square of patched fabric – I used four coordinating prints to create mine

46cm (½yd) plain fabric for the back and border

41cm (16in) pillow pad

285cm (112in) of 5mm (¼in) wide piping cord (if you want to make your own, see the video link on page 46)

1 Cut your patterned fabric into nine 11cm (4¼in) squares. (I chose 11cm/4¼in to fit the print of my fabric). Sew together in rows of three, then sew these three strips together to make a square.

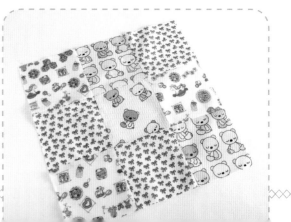

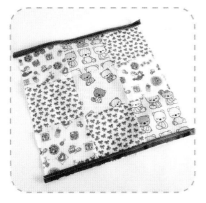

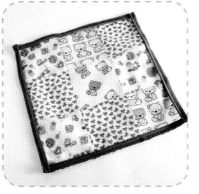

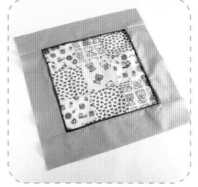

2 With the zipper foot on your machine, sew piping to the top and bottom of the patchwork square, raw edges together.

3 Sew piping to the remaining two sides – snip away a little of the cord from the ends of these strips to help reduce bulk in the corners.

4 Cut four strips of plain fabric measuring 10 x 43cm (4 x 17in). Sew a strip to opposite sides of the patchworked square, centrally, right sides together. Press open, then sew on the top and bottom pieces in the same way. Trim the square down to 42cm (16½in).

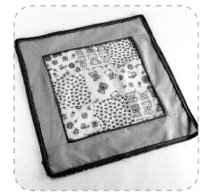

Tip
Appliqué letters spelling baby's name would make this pillow a perfect gift!

5 Apply piping cord around the edge of the square; snip into the corners of the tape as you sew, so that the fabric lies flat, and overlap the ends when they meet.

6 Cut two pieces of plain fabric measuring 42 x 56cm (16½ x 22in). Fold in half, with the short ends together, and press. Place these two pieces over the patchworked piece, right sides facing, overlapping each other, and with raw edges together. Pin then sew around the whole shape.

7 Remove the pins, snip across the corners, turn right side out and press. Insert your pillow pad.

Laundry Bin

Whether it's for laundry or toys, this handy bin will help to keep the nursery tidy. Create cute appliqué shapes by using baby's hands as templates – little feet would work just as well!

Tip

Beginner sewers may find it easier to leave off the piping trim.

Finished size

33 x 43cm (13 x 17in)

What you need

94 x 66cm (37 x 26in) single-sided fusible foam stabiliser

96.5 x 35.5cm (38 x 14in) outer fabric

96.5 x 91.5cm (38 x 36in) lining fabric

96.5cm (38in) piping trim (mine was shop-bought, to make your own see step 1, page 62 or the video link on page 46)

102cm (40in) of 3mm (1/8in) wide ribbon

Bodkin or safety pin

Fusible webbing

Cut

Cut the foam stabiliser to 94 x 33cm (37 x 13in)

Cut a circle of foam stabiliser measuring 30.5cm (12in) across

Cut the outer fabric to 96.5 x 35.5cm (38 x 14in)

Cut a piece of lining fabric to 96.5 x 35.5cm (38 x 14in)

Cut two circles of lining fabric measuring 33cm (13in) across

Cut a strip of lining fabric measuring 96.5 x 23cm (38 x 9in)

Cut two pieces of lining fabric for the handles measuring 10 x 20.5cm (4 x 8in)

1 Sew the piping trim across the long top edge of the outer fabric, right sides together.

2 Take the 96.5 x 23cm (38 x 9in) strip of lining fabric, fold each short end over by 1cm (½in) twice, and sew. Repeat with the top edge – this will form the channel for the ribbon tie to thread through. Sew this strip centrally to the top of the outer fabric, right sides facing and aligning raw edges, using the zipper foot on your machine. You'll notice the top panel is slightly shorter than the fabric.

3 Draw around baby's hand onto paper, then cut out to make a template. Iron the fusible webbing onto the back of a piece of lining fabric, then cut out the shape.

4 Peel away the paper backing, position the appliqué hands on the outer fabric and iron in place. Free-motion embroider a couple of times around the edge.

5 Repeat with as many hands as you wish!

6 Fold the short ends of the two 10 x 20.5cm (4 x 8in) pieces of lining fabric over by 1cm (½in) and press, then fold the two long sides to the centre and press again. Fold in half and sew all the way round the outside edge to make two handles.

7 Sew the handles in place 15.25cm (6in) from each side, and 2.5cm (1in) under the piping.

8 Fuse the 94 x 33cm (37 x 13in) foam stabiliser centrally to the back of the outer strip. Fold the strip right sides together and sew up the short ends to create a 'tube' of fabric.

9 Fuse the circle of foam stabiliser centrally to the wrong side of one of the circles.

10 Pin or clip this circle to the base of the bin, with right sides facing in.

11 Carefully sew all the way round the base, then turn right side out.

12 Sew the short ends of the remaining lining strip right sides together to make a tube, leave a turning gap of about 15.25cm (6in). Sew the circular base in place in the same way as for the outer fabrics. Drop the outer bin inside the lining with the right sides together, and sew around the top with the zipper foot on your machine. Turn right side out and sew the turning gap closed. Push the lining inside the bin.

13 Thread the ribbon through the channel using your bodkin or safety pin, then tie.

Nursery Storage

This useful hanging storage unit will coordinate with your nursery decor, and can make use of potential storage space on the back of a door or inside a closet. Nappies/diapers and wipes don't tend to come in pretty packaging so hide them, and as you can easily see what's in here you know when you need to restock!

Finished size

30.5 x 66cm (12 x 26in)

What you need

94 x 63.5cm (37 x 25in) yellow fabric
97.5 x 30.5cm (38½ x 12in) grey fabric
99 x 36.75cm (39 x 14.5in) wadding/batting
30.5cm (12in) of 5mm (¼in) piping cord (see also the video link on page 46)
Child's coat hanger
45.75cm (18in) of 1cm (½in) wide ribbon and 45.75cm (18in) of 2.5cm (1in) wide lace, tied in a bow around the hanger hook
28cm (11in) of 5mm (¼in) wide elastic
Safety pin or bodkin
Three decorative buttons
Erasable ink pen and ruler

1 Cut a strip of grey fabric measuring 4 x 30.5cm (1½ x 12in). Wrap this around the piping cord with the raw edges wrong sides together and sew with the zipper foot on your sewing machine.

2 Cut four pieces of yellow fabric, two measuring 27 x 30.5cm (10½ x 12in) and two measuring 31.75 x 63.5cm (12½ x 25in). Fold the larger pieces in half, short ends together. Measure and mark 2.5cm (1in) in from each side edge, then trim down from the top along the sides, gently tapering the shape.

3 Place the large piece of fabric and one small piece on top of the wadding/batting – don't trim the wadding/batting to size just yet. Using your ruler and erasable ink pen, draw a diagonal 4cm (1½in) grid across both pieces.

4 Sew across the lines to quilt, then trim the wadding/batting to size.

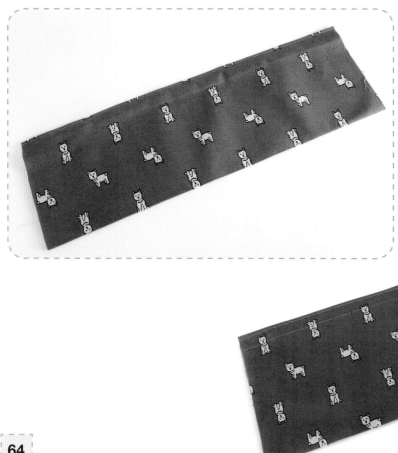

5 For the pockets, cut two pieces of grey fabric measuring 38 x 15.25cm (15 x 6in), and two measuring 35.5 x 12.75cm (14 x 5in). Sew each pair right sides together along the long sides, then turn the tubes right side out and press. Topstitch along the top edge of the longer pocket.

6 Topstitch across the top of the deeper pocket, then sew a second row of stitches 1cm (½in) below.

7 Thread the elastic onto your bodkin or safety pin, then pass through the channel you've just created across the top of the pocket. Pull gently, then tack/baste the end of the elastic to the pocket to stop it pulling through.

8 Sew both sides of this pocket to the small quilted section of yellow fabric, 12.75cm (5in) from the top. Don't pull the elastic too tight or the backing fabric will curl.

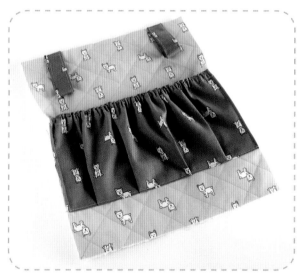

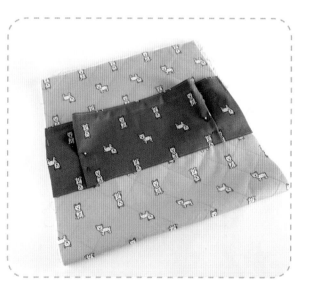

9 Form the bottom of the pocket into four even pleats to make it the same width as the fabric, then sew. Cut two strips of grey fabric measuring 10 x 18cm (4 x 7in), fold in half lengthways then fold the raw edges to the centre. Fold in half to create 2.5cm (1in) wide straps. Topstitch along each long edge. Tack/baste these, folded in half, facing inwards to the top of the yellow fabric, 5cm (2in) from each side.

10 Sew the sides of the second pocket to the larger quilted piece, 10cm (4in) from the top, while it is unfolded. Pin two pleats evenly along the bottom, approximately 5cm (2in) from each side, and sew across the bottom of the pocket.

11 Mark the centre of the pocket and sew to divide into two. Add a decorative button to the centre (again, sew while the main fabric is unfolded).

12 Sew the strip of piping to the top of this section, with the raw edges aligned (again, sew while the main fabric is unfolded).

13 Take the section with the elasticated pocket and sew right sides together with the matching piece of yellow fabric, leaving the bottom edge open. Turn right side out, then fold the raw edge inwards by about 1cm (½in); press.

14 Sew the large quilted piece right sides together with the remaining large piece of yellow fabric along both long sides. Turn right side out and press, then topstitch along the two long sides.

15 Fold the long piece so that the top edges meet and tack/baste them together. Slip this inside the top section of the unit, then tack/baste. Topstitch all around the top section, securing the bottom section as you sew along the bottom edge. Add a couple of buttons to the base of the straps to finish.

16 Tie the ribbon and lace around the hanger hook, then hang up your nursery storage!

Tip
Make the top section longer and add more pockets for extra storage!

Stroller Bag

VIDEO

Making a
letterbox zip

This handy bag is large enough to carry baby's important things on a day out: nappies/diapers, bottles, feeding equipment and toys. The elasticated side pockets keep drinks to hand and there's zippered pockets on both the front flap and back of the bag to secure items like your purse or phone. Hook the bag over the handles of your stroller, or attach the longer strap and carry the bag over your shoulder!

Finished size

58.5 x 30.5 x 12.75cm (23 x 12 x 5in)

What you need

75 x 114cm (29½ x 45in) large print fabric

1m x 114cm (39½ x 45in) small print fabric

1.5m (1²/₃yd) lining fabric

1m (1yd) square wadding/batting

30cm (12.5in) of 1in (½in) wide hook-and-loop fastening tape

Magnetic clasp

30.5cm (12in) of 1cm (½in) wide elastic

45.75cm (18in) zip

25.5cm (10in) zip

Four metal bag feet

43 x 12.75cm (17 x 5in) mesh bag base

Repositionable spray fabric adhesive

Marking pen

Safety pin or bodkin

10cm (4in) circle template

Cutting list

For the bag back and front, cut two large-print fabric pieces, two lining pieces and two wadding/batting pieces, each measuring 44.5 x 33cm (17½ x 13in)

For the sides, cut two large-print pieces, two lining pieces and two wadding/batting pieces, each measuring 12.75 x 33cm (5 x 13in)

For the base, cut one large-print piece, one lining piece and one wadding/batting piece, each measuring 44.5 x 12.75cm (17½ x 5in)

For the bag flap, cut one small-print piece of fabric, one lining piece and one wadding/batting piece, each measuring 43 x 35.5cm (17 x 14in)

For the bag flap pocket, cut two lining pieces, each measuring 30.5cm (12in) square

For the elasticated side pockets, cut one small-print fabric piece, one lining piece and one wadding/batting piece, each measuring 25.5 x 28cm (10 x 11in), then one small-print piece, one lining piece and one wadding/batting piece, each measuring 25.5 x 20.5cm (10 x 8in)

For the outer back pocket, cut two small-print fabric pieces measuring 44.5 x 16.5cm (17½ x 6½in) and two small-print fabric pieces measuring 44.5 x 6.5cm (17½ x 2½in)

The inside pockets are two strips of small-print fabric and two of lining, each measuring 61 x 20.5cm (24 x 8in)

For the side straps, cut four pieces of small-print fabric and two wadding/batting pieces, each measuring 10 x 30.5cm (4 x 12in)

The shoulder strap is made of two pieces of large-print fabric and one wadding/batting piece, each measuring 10 x 76.25cm (4 x 30in) (make them longer if you wish)

1 First make up the elasticated side pockets. Fuse the wadding/batting to the wrong sides of the outer pieces of fabric with spray adhesive. Sew the tops of the pockets right sides together with the linings. Turn over right side out and press. Topstitch across the seam, then sew another line a little over 1cm (½in) below the first, to create a channel for the elastic. Cut the elastic in half and feed through the channel with the help of a safety pin.

2 Gently pull the elastic through the channel. When the end of the elastic meets the fabric, tack/baste to secure. Pull the elastic until the gathered section measures 12.75cm (5in). Tack/baste the other end in place and trim away the excess elastic.

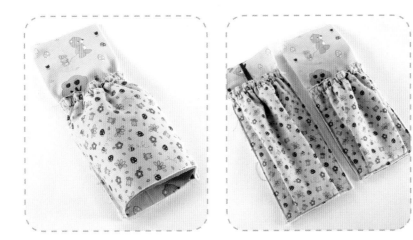

3 Fuse the wadding/batting to the wrong side of the outer side panels. Place the elasticated pocket over the side panel and sew along the sides. The bottom of the pocket will be wider than the side panel.

4 Make two pleats in the base of each pocket, 2.5cm (1in) from each side, and sew. You should have two side panels that look like this.

5 To make up the flap, fuse the wadding/batting to the wrong side of the outer fabric and round off the bottom corners using your circle template. Round off the bottom corners of the lining as well.

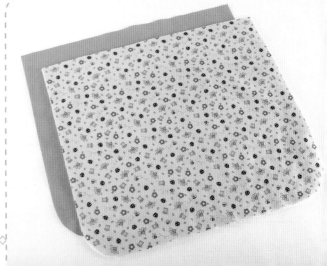

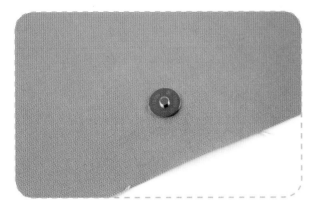

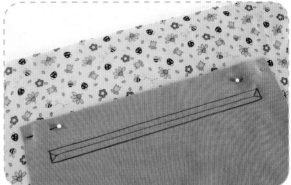

6 Apply the thinner side of the magnetic clasp to the centre of the lining, 4cm (1½in) up from the bottom edge (see applying magnetic clasps on page 13).

7 Pin one half of the flap pocket fabric to the centre of the right side of the outer fabric, with the bottom edges meeting. Draw a box, 4cm (1½in) down from the top and centrally, measuring 23 x 1cm (9 x ½in). Draw a line along the middle of the box and form a 'Y' shape at each end.

8 Sew around the outside of the rectangle. With a small pair of scissors, cut along the central line and into the 'Y' corners, being very careful not to cut through the stitches!

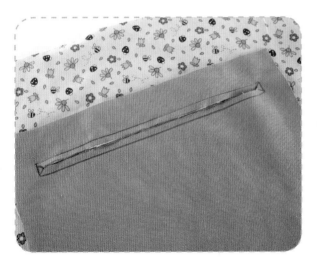

9 'Post' the lining through the hole and press.

10 Take the 25.5cm (10in) zip and tack/baste behind the hole. Sewing the open ends of the zip together first by hand helps. From the right side, sew around the zip. Remove the tacking/basting stitches.

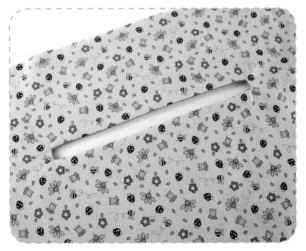

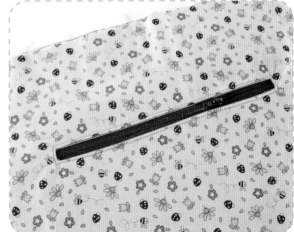

11 Turn the flap over to the wrong side.

12 Pin the second side of the pocket fabric to the first, right sides facing, then sew the two pieces together around all four edges, without sewing through the patterned flap fabric.

13 Remove the pins. Place the flap lining right sides together with the outer section, then sew all the way round leaving the top open. Snip around the curves with pinking shears.

14 Turn right side out and press. Topstitch around the sides and bottom edge.

15 Now to make up the zipped back pocket. The smaller strips (6.5cm/2½in deep) will make up the top of the pocket and the larger pieces (16.5cm/6½in deep) will be the bottom.

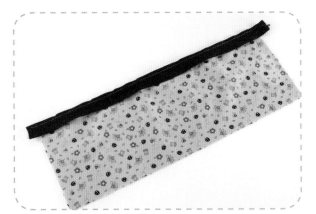

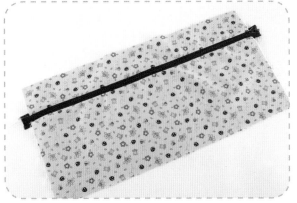

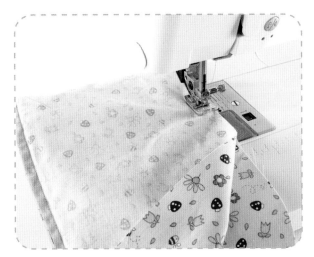

16 Place the 45.75cm (18in) zip face down over the top of one large strip, aligning the raw edges, and sew. Flip the fabric back and press.

17 Sew a smaller strip to the top side of the zip in the same way; flip open and press.

18 Repeat to attach the two remaining strips onto the back of the zip.

19 Fold the two larger fabric pieces right sides together, with the zip in between and sew the long edge.

20 Turn this tube right side out. Do the same with the shorter strips – you'll need to roll the larger section out of the way.

21 Turn the tube right side out and press. Topstitch along each side of the zip, then trim away any excess zip.

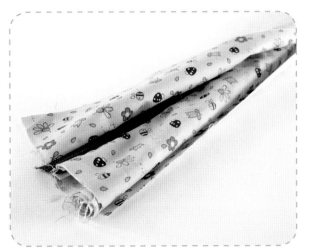

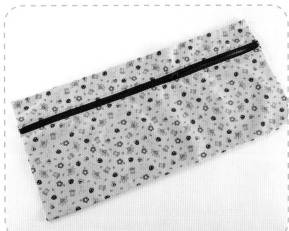

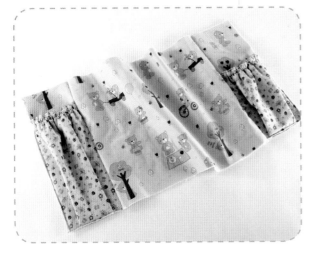

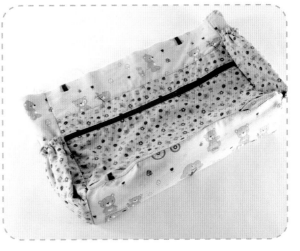

22 Fuse the wadding/batting to the wrong side of the front, back and base outer fabrics. Sew the side panels to the front of the bag, right sides together.

23 Pin the back zipped pocket to the back bag fabric, 4cm (1½in) from the bottom of the bag and sew across the top and bottom of the pocket. Sew in the back panel to make a tube with the front and side pieces, then sew in the base. Turn right side out.

24 Cut the mesh to the size of the interior bag base and insert into the bag. Make small incisions 2.5cm (1in) from each corner and push the bag feet into each corner, through both the fabric and mesh base.

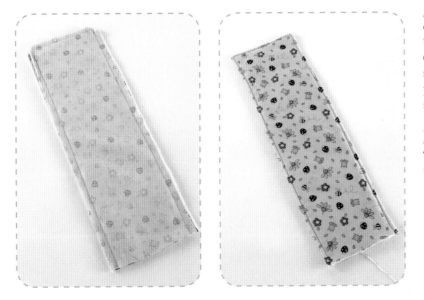

25 To make the side straps, fuse the wadding/batting to two pieces of outer fabric. Sew these right sides together with the remaining pieces, leaving the bottom short side open. Snip across the corners.

26 Turn right side out and press. Topstitch around the edges, leaving the bottom edge open.

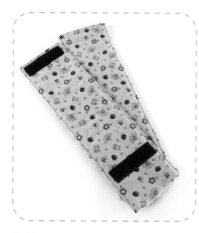

27 Cut the hook-and-loop fastener into 7cm (2¾in) strips, sew one 'fluffy' piece close to the sewn end of each tab, and a 'hook' piece 5cm (2in) from the opposite end.

28 Make up the shoulder strap by fusing the wadding/batting to the back of one fabric piece, then sew the two strap pieces right sides together, leaving a turning gap of about 10cm (4in) in one side. Snip off the corners, turn right side out and press. Topstitch all the way around. Offer the ends of the strap to the side tabs and mark the position of the hook-and-loop fastenings, then sew the corresponding pieces in place on the strap – make sure the hooks match up with the loops, as shown!

29 Pin the flap right sides together to the top of the back of the bag and sew, do the same with the side straps to the sides of the bag, with the hook-and-loop sections facing downwards. Remove the pins.

30 Now for the inside pockets. Sew each piece of outer fabric right sides together with a piece of lining, across the long top edge. Fold over and press, topstitch along the seam.

31 Sew the sides of the pockets to the sides of the front and back lining pieces. Mark the centre of the pocket and sew along this line.

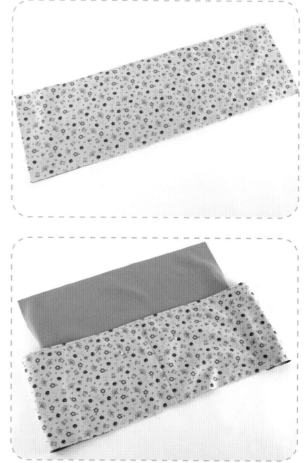

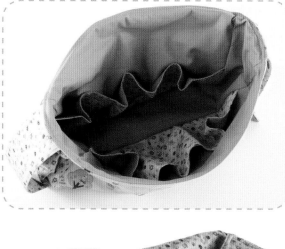

32 Mark the centre of each side of the pocket and sew to make four pockets. Pleat the bottom of the pockets evenly to the width of the base of the lining and sew.

33 Sew the sides, front and back lining pieces right sides together as you did with the outer bag, but this time leave a turning gap of about 10cm (4in) in one side. Sew in the base. Drop the outer bag inside the lining, right sides together, and sew around the top.

34 Turn right side out and press. Sew the turning gap closed, then push the lining inside the bag. Topstitch around the top edge to finish.

Here's your finished bag from the front...

... and the back!

Stroller Sleeping Bag

Keep baby cosy and warm in this fleecy, lined sleeping bag, with seatbelt holes to keep him safe! The measurements below should fit a baby up to about 1 year of age; for a toddler add an extra 20.5cm (8in) to the length.

Finished size

53.5 x 91.5cm (21 x 36in)

What you need

One piece of outer fleece measuring 102 x 96.5cm (40 x 38in)

One piece of lining fleece measuring 102 x 96.5cm (40 x 38in)

One piece of wadding/batting measuring 112 x 96.5cm (44 x 38in)

51 x 84cm (20 x 33in) scrap fabric or paper and marking tool to make a template

76.25cm (30in) zip

Repositionable spray adhesive

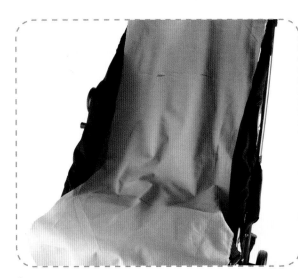

1 Push your scrap piece of fabric or paper into the back of the stroller and mark the position of the seatbelt straps.

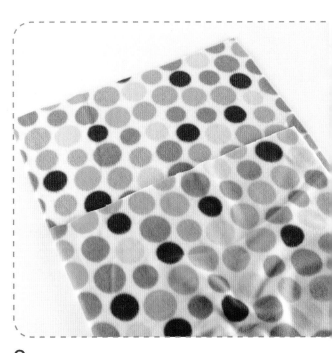

2 Fold your outer piece of fabric in half widthways. At the centre fold, cut down 30.5cm (12in) from the top, then cut out to the right-hand edge through the top layer of fabric only. You will now have a large 'L' shape of fabric. Repeat for the lining fabric.

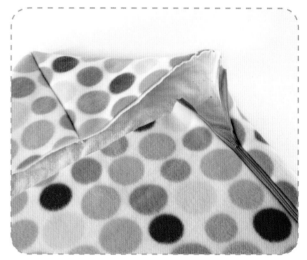

3 Transfer the seatbelt markings from your template to the centre back of the lining fleece, starting with the shoulder straps, 30.5cm (12in) from the top.

4 Attach the outer fleece wrong sides together with the wadding/batting with a little repositionable spray adhesive, then trim the wadding/batting to shape. Fold the top part of the fleece in half, right sides together, and sew to form a hood. Fold the top part of the blanket lining in half right sides together and sew in the same way to form a hood.

5 Sew the zip to the open side of the outer sleeping bag.

6 Sew the lining fleece to the opposite side of the zip tape, so that the zip is sandwiched in between the two layers of fleece.

7 Sew the hood lining and outer sections right sides together. When you come to sew the end of the zip, tuck the end of the tape into the seam.

8 Sew straight across the bottom of the sleeping bag, leaving a turning gap in the lining fleece of about 15.25cm (6in). Push the zip towards the lining side as you sew. Make sure the zip is open.

9 Turn the whole bag right side out then sew the opening closed. Push the lining inside the bag. Make a few hand stitches in the point of the hood to hold the lining and outer fleece layers together.

10 Use a long or endless buttonhole stitch on your machine to sew through both layers of fleece over your original seatbelt marks. If you don't have a buttonhole stitch on your machine, sew two rows of satin stitch. Cut along the marks.

11 Thread the seat belt straps through the slits and you're ready to go!

Tip

You could hand sew a blanket stitch around the slits if you prefer – this is quite easy on fleece as the fabric won't fray.

Travel Changing Mat

This simple-to-make tote will prove really handy when you're
out and about. Its wipe-clean mat and handy nappy/diaper
pouch will make it easy to change baby anywhere!

Finished size

When open, 37 x 74cm (14½ x 29in)

What you need

81.25 x 63.5cm (32 x 25in) outer fabric

43 x 38cm (17 x 15in) lining fabric

81.25 x 63.5cm (32 x 25in) high-loft wadding/batting

41 x 61cm (16 x 24in) soft vinyl (you could laminate your own fabric with iron-on vinyl if you prefer, or replace with towelling)

132cm (52in) of 2.5cm (1in) wide webbing

Magnetic clasp

Non-stick foot for your machine

Clear nylon thread

Cut

For the flap, cut one fabric piece, one wadding/batting piece and one vinyl piece, each measuring 41 x 61cm (16 x 24in)

For the pocket, cut two fabric pieces, two lining pieces and two wadding/batting pieces, each measuring 43 x 19cm (17 x 7½in)

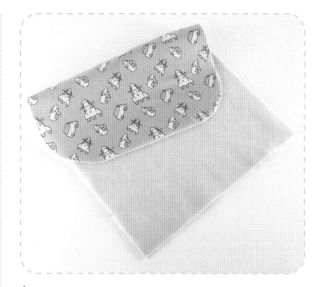

1 Cut a curve from the top two corners of the flap fabric, wadding/batting and vinyl. Adhere the wadding/batting to the wrong side of the fabric.

2 Sew the vinyl right sides together with the fabric, leaving the short straight side open. Snip around the curves, turn right side out and press from the fabric side, so as not to melt the vinyl. Topstitch 2.5cm (1in) from the hemmed edge. (You'll find it easier to use a non-stick foot and sew with the vinyl side up.)

3 Fuse the wadding/batting to the wrong sides of the outer pocket pieces. Cut a 43cm (17in) length of webbing and tack/baste to each side of the front of the pocket, 6cm (2½in) from the top.

Tip

Use clear nylon thread in the top of your machine when topstitching the vinyl to make it truly wipe-clean; some vinyl will 'heal' the stitchholes when heat is applied.

4 Sew the pocket pieces right sides together, leaving the top edge open. Pinch the bottom corners so that the side seams meet the bottom seam and sew across the corners, 2.5cm (1in) from the points. This will make the base of the bag square.

5 Repeat with the lining pieces, but this time leave a turning gap of about 25.5cm (10in) in the base. (This is an extra-wide turning gap as the whole mat will have to be pulled through it.)

6 Turn the outer bag right side out. Tack/baste the ends of the remaining webbing length, facing downwards, to each side seam.

7 Push the mat, vinyl side down, under the webbing across the pocket and tack/baste centrally to the top of the bag.

8 Fit the magnetic clasp centrally to the lining, 2.5cm (1in) from the top (see page 13).

9 Roll up the mat and push the outer pocket inside the lining, right sides facing. Sew around the top, making sure the strap is tucked inside.

10 Turn right side out and press. Sew the opening closed, then push the lining inside the pocket. Topstitch around the top.

11 Fold the mat over the pocket and thread under the webbing.

12 Fold the mat over the pocket again, and tuck under the webbing strap.

Quiet Cube

This simple cube is actually an educational toy! Let's count, touch and learn colours. I've used a mixture of cotton and felt; you could attach a square of fleece or towelling to add more texture to the cube, and make it in any size you like!

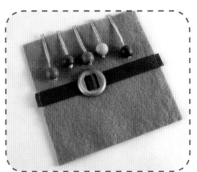

1 Fold each 10cm (4in) strip of ribbon in half, and tack/baste five of the ribbons along one side of two fabric squares.

2 Thread and knot the five different buttons onto bakers' twine; tack/baste the twine to each side of the remaining fabric square.

3 Thread the 1cm (½in) wide strip of ribbon through the buckle and tack/baste to each side of one of the felt squares. Using a large-eyed needle, thread 5mm (¼in) wide ribbon through five of the wooden beads individually and knot the ends. Put a little wet glue behind each knot to make sure the beads can't pull off. Tack/baste these to one side of the felt square.

4 Sew the seven different coloured buttons in the shape of a flower in the centre of a felt square. Secure the thread with a dot of wet glue on the back of the fabric.

5 Thread an 18cm (7in) length of the 5mm (¼in) wide ribbon through the remaining five beads. Tack/baste to each side of the third piece of felt.

6 Sew four of the panels right sides together to form a strip (I alternated felt and fabric). Use a small stitch to strengthen the seams.

7 Sew the two ends right sides together, then sew the top and bottom squares in to make the cube, leaving a turning gap in one side of about 10cm (4in). Turn right side out, stuff with toy filler, then hand sew the opening closed.

Cot Quilt

This sleeping teddy is a cute bedtime buddy for baby! This is the perfect project for the beginner quilter, as you can't go too far wrong with squares. Each of my finished squares measures 9.5cm (3¾in) – you could use the same total amount of fabric but make the squares larger or smaller if you wish.

1 Take a look at the wadding/ batting manufacturer's instructions, – you may need to prewash it if it's likely to shrink. Cut your fat quarters into 11cm (4¼in) squares. (You will have a few too many.)

2 Join together a row of seven squares. Now repeat.

Finished size

81.25 x 117cm (32 x 46in)

What you need

For the patchworked area, four fat quarters of coordinating fabrics

For the border, 127 x 45.75cm (50 x 18in) fabric

For the top end of the quilt, 68.5 x 30.5cm (27 x 12in) plain fabric

419cm (165in) of 2.5cm (1in) wide bias binding (I made my own, see how on page 12)

406cm (160in) of 5mm (¼in) piping cord

406cm (160in) of 2.5cm (1in) wide bias-cut tape (I used the same as my bias binding)

41 x 51cm (16 x 20in) of brown fabric for the bear

Two 15.25cm (6in) squares of lighter fabric for the nose

68.5 x 15.25cm (27 x 6in) interfacing

91.5 x 127cm (36 x 50in) backing fabric

91.5 x 127cm (36 x 50in) premium quilt wadding/ batting

23cm (9in), 12.75cm (5in) and 9cm (3½in) circle templates and marking tool

Approximately 50g (1¾oz) toy filler

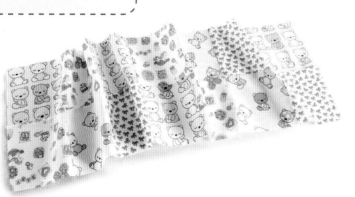

3 When you have nine rows of seven, sew these together in turn, making sure the seams match as you sew.

4 Cut a wavy line across the top of the patchwork fabric.

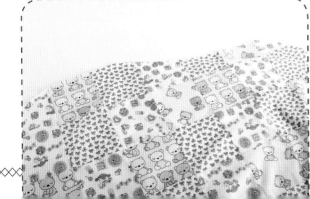

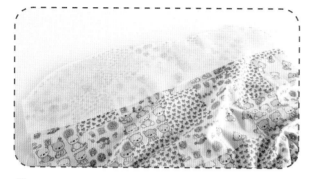

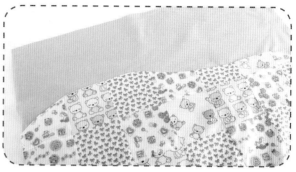

5 Cut a 15.25cm (6in) strip of interfacing, and sew to the right side of the wavy edge.

6 Snip into the curves, turn right side out and press. Pin, then topstitch this piece to the plain fabric along the wavy edge. Remove the pins. Trim the plain fabric to the same width as the patchwork.

7 To make up the bear face, use your 23cm (9in) template and marking tool to draw a circle on brown fabric. Use the 9cm (3½in) template to add two ears. The 12.75cm (5in) template is used to create a circular muzzle from lighter fabric. Cut two of each shape. For the paw, cut two 9 x 10cm (3½ x 4in) pieces of brown fabric and use the 9cm (3½in) circle template to round off one end of each piece. Draw two semi-circles for sleepy eyes; a triangle and 'W' shape make up the nose and mouth on the lighter fabric.

8 Sew the nose and mouth onto the muzzle using a triple straight stitch on your machine. Sew the muzzle circles right sides together all the way round. Snip into the seam allowance, then make a small cut of about 5cm (2in) into the back and turn right side out. Press. Insert a little toy filler to give the nose some shape, then topstitch onto the centre of the face.

9 Sew the sleeping eyes with a triple straight stitch. Sew the two face pieces right sides together. Snip into the seam allowance. Make a cut in the back of the face of about 10cm (4in) and turn right side out. Pop a little toy filler inside.

10 Make the paw in the same way: sew right sides together, then make a cut of about 5cm (2in) in the back and turn right side out. Insert the toy filler. Draw then sew a couple of 4cm (1½in) lines to form toes. Pin the head and paw over the wavy edge of the patchwork squares. Topstitch in place, then remove the pins.

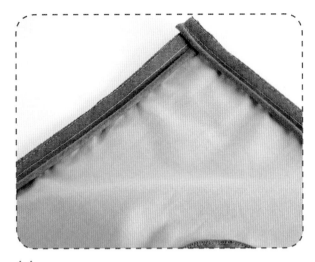

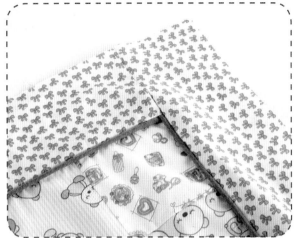

11 Make the piping by folding the 2.5cm (1in) bias-cut tape of fabric around the piping cord, wrong sides facing (see the video link on page 46). Sew the cord in place with the zipper foot on your machine. Trim the seam allowance to 5mm (¼in). Sew the raw edge of the piping to the right side of the quilt one edge at a time. When you come to the corners, pull the cord and trim 1cm (½in) from the end so that there isn't a bulky corner.

12 Cut the border fabric into strips 9cm (3½in) wide. With the zipper foot still on your machine, sew right side together with the quilt top, as close to the cord as you can. Sew strips across the top and bottom first, then sew two long strips along either side; press.

13 Place the quilt top over the wadding/batting, then the whole piece in turn on top of the wrong side of the backing fabric.

14 Secure with pins, then 'stitch in the ditch' (sew along the seams) around the squares through all layers to quilt. Remove the pins.

15 Trim any excess backing fabric and wadding/batting to the size of the quilt top. Apply bias tape all around the edge. I prefer to machine sew the tape to the right side then hand sew on the back, mitring the corners. It's quite time-consuming, but worth it!

Burp Cloths

These oh-so-useful burp cloths help to protect your clothing from dribbles, and are soft and snuggly for baby to rest her cheek on. The handy pouch is perfect for travelling – you could easily fit a nappy/diaper in one side. As one of the simplest projects in this book, even a beginner sewer can make this useful gift for a newborn.

Finished size

Finished size of cloths:
28 x 49.5cm (11 x 19½in)

Finished size of pouch when closed: 23 x 19cm (9 x 7½in)

What you need

68.5 x 74cm (27 x 29in) soft towelling fabric

68.5 x 89cm (27 x 35in) fabric

68.5 x 23cm (27 x 9in) wadding/batting

127cm (50in) of 1cm (½in) wide bias binding

76.25cm (30in) of 3mm (⅛in) wide ribbon to tie (optional)

Magnetic clasp

1 To make the two burp cloths, cut two pieces of towelling measuring 25.5 x 51cm (10 x 20in) and two pieces of fabric measuring 33 x 56cm (13 x 22in). Sew the long sides of the towelling pieces right sides together with the long sides of the fabric.

2 Flatten the tube so that the fabric border on each side is even, then sew across each end, leaving a turning gap of about 10cm (4in) in one seam. Turn right side out and press, then topstitch all around the edge, closing the turning gap.

3 To make the pouch, cut one piece of fabric, one piece of wadding/batting and one towelling piece, each measuring 68.5 x 23cm (27 x 9in). Place the wadding/batting over the wrong side of the fabric. Fold each short end over by 15.25cm (6in). Measure 2.5cm (1in) from the fold, and mark this position centrally. Apply one half of the magnetic clasp to each mark. Make sure you only fix the clasp to one layer of wadding/batting backed fabric.

4 Place the towelling over the wadding/batting. Sew a strip of bias binding over each short edge.

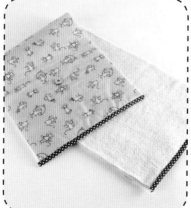

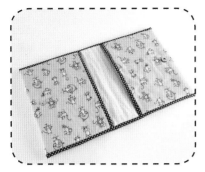

5 Fold the short ends of the fabric over again by 15.25cm (6in), with the towelling on the inside. Apply bias binding along both long sides, folding the ends of the tape around the edge of the fabric to make neat.

6 Pop the burp cloths inside.

Templates

All the templates are given at actual size. Simply trace them off.

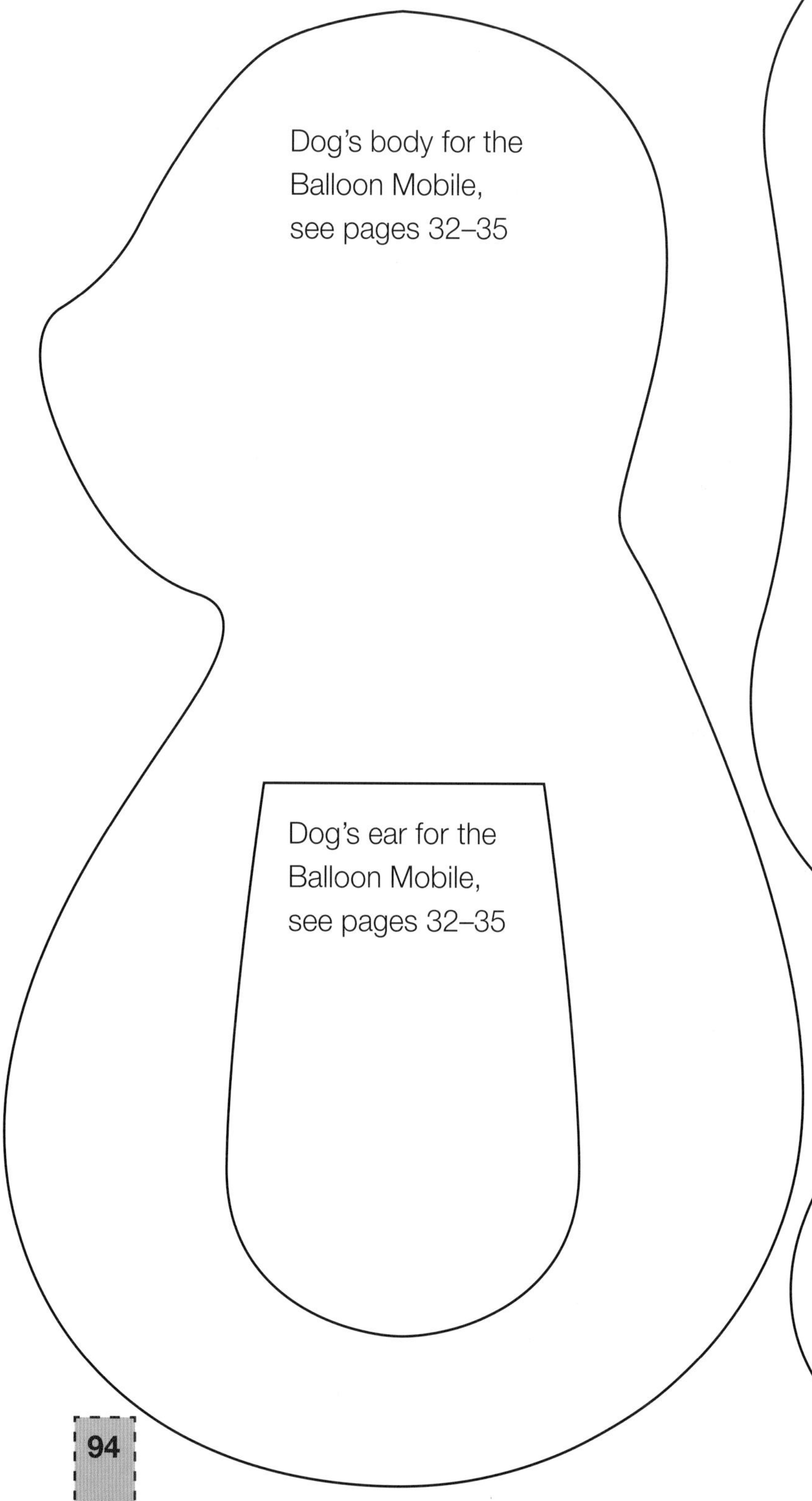

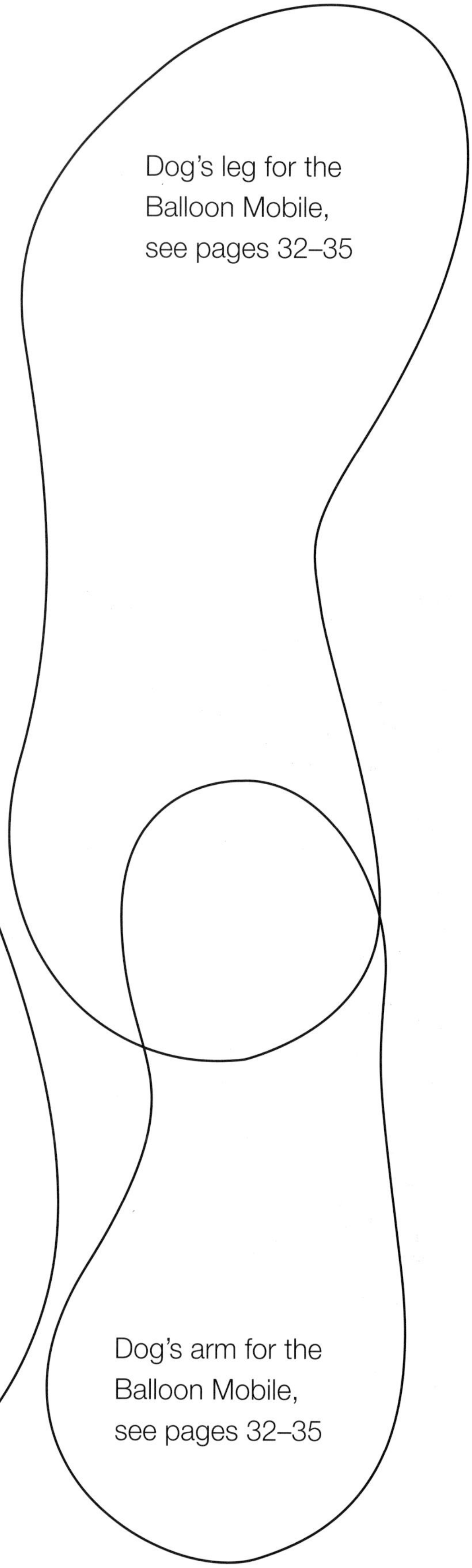

Dog's body for the
Balloon Mobile,
see pages 32–35

Dog's leg for the
Balloon Mobile,
see pages 32–35

Dog's ear for the
Balloon Mobile,
see pages 32–35

Dog's arm for the
Balloon Mobile,
see pages 32–35

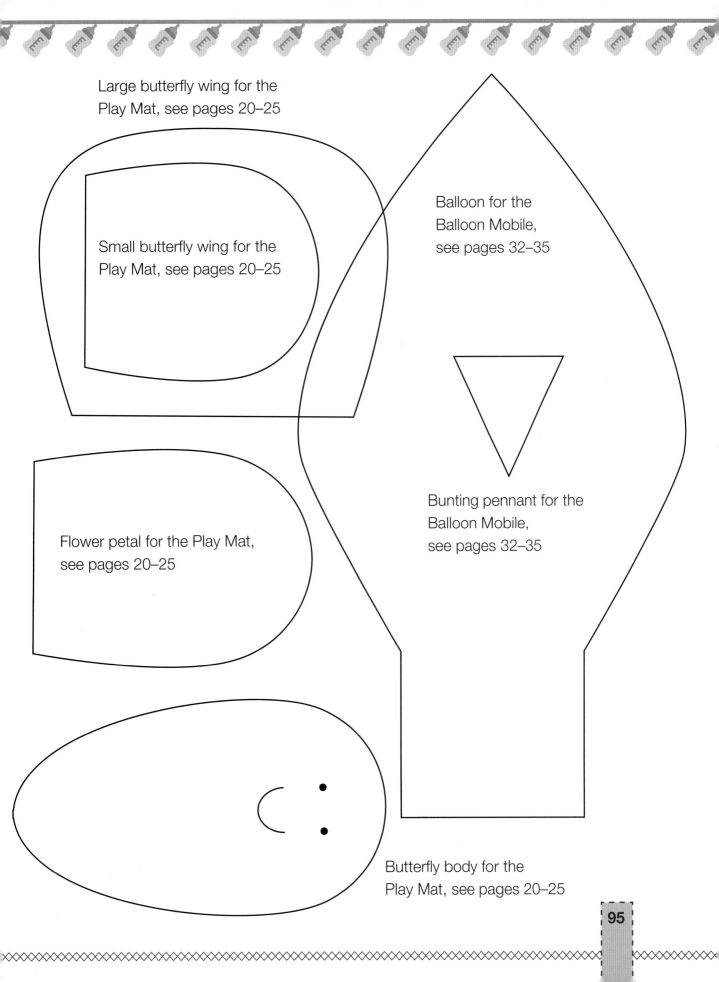

Large butterfly wing for the
Play Mat, see pages 20–25

Small butterfly wing for the
Play Mat, see pages 20–25

Balloon for the
Balloon Mobile,
see pages 32–35

Flower petal for the Play Mat,
see pages 20–25

Bunting pennant for the
Balloon Mobile,
see pages 32–35

Butterfly body for the
Play Mat, see pages 20–25

Index

QR-CODED VIDEOS:

Cutting and folding bias binding 12
Continuous bias binding 12
Applying bias binding 13
Deconstructing a Moses basket 26
Making a baby nest 42
Piping 46
Making a letterbox zip 68